TELEVISION IN THE MAKING

CONTENTS

Pattern of Marriage, The Declining Years, Children in Trust, Return to Living, The New Canadians, Can I Have a Lawyer?, Those Who Dare. Now with Associated-Rediffusion Ltd.

DOCUMENTARY TV JOURNALISM by Norman Swallow

Joined the B.B.C. in 1946 as writer-producer of sound radio features. Transferred to television in 1950, first as Talks producer and then in Documentary department. First television programme was *An American Looks at Britain* with Howard K. Smith, of C.B.S., and Ed. Newman, of N.B.C. Started *Special Enquiry* series in 1952 as an experiment in television journalism; the series is still running. Producer since 1954 of *The World is Ours* series made in collaboration with the United Nations. Now with B.B.C. Talks department.

OUTSIDE TELEVISION BROADCASTS by Peter Dimmock

After war service and brief spell as a journalist, Peter Dimmock joined the B.B.C. Television Outside Broadcast Unit as producer-commentator, specializing in sports events. In 1947 he brought Royal Ascot to the television screen for the first time; since then has either produced or commentated several hundred outside broadcasts, including the Olympic Games, 1948, the first television Boat Race, 1949, the funeral of King George VI and the Coronation Ceremony from Westminster Abbey, 1953. Initiated *Sportsview* in 1954. Now Head of B.B.C. Television Outside Broadcasts.

BALLET, OPERA AND MUSIC by Philip Bate

Joined the B.B.C. in 1934 as liaison between Drama and Music Departments in sound radio. Transferred to television first as stage-manager in 1937, then as producer. After war service, surveyed music resources for television in 1946 and became Music Producer when B.B.C. service re-opened after the war. Originated the *Conductor Speaks* series with Sir Henry Wood and the *Ballet for Beginners* series. Now producer with B.B.C. Television Music Department.

VARIETY AND TELEVISION by Max Liebman

Involved in American show-business, movies, musicals and revues since 1920, Liebman entered American television in 1949 as producer of *Your Show of Shows*, a 90-minute revue for N.B.C. every Saturday night. The series gained him many awards and introduced such stars as Sid Caesar, Imogene Coca, Marguerite Piazza. He also produced Bob Hope's television debut and the Elgin-American Thanksgiving Day show with Milton Berle, George Jessel and the Ritz Brothers. His latest series for N.B.C., known as *Spectaculars*, is in colour; begun in 1954, it includes *Lady in the Dark, Best Foot Forward, Babes in Toyland, The Connecticut Yankee* and *The Merry Widow*, using such talent as Betty Hutton, Judy Holliday, Frank Sinatra, Sonja Henje, Martha Raye, Nelson Eddy, etc.

TELEVISION FOR CHILDREN by Michael Westmore

Producer for five years of many B.B.C. television programmes for children and teen-agers, becoming known for *Whirligig, Saturday Special, Jig-Saw, All Your Own* and *Tele-club*. Now in charge of children's programmes for Associated-Rediffusion Ltd.

Entered film industry in 1932 as assistant-director and unit manager at Shepperton Studios, specializing in foreign location work. Joined the B.B.C. in 1938 as producer in Outside Broadcast Unit. After war service, rejoined B.B.C. Television and was appointed Newsreel Manager in 1947, helping to launch *TV Newsreel* in 1948. Now with B.B.C. Television Outside Broadcasts department.

Played many major roles in the London theatre such as *Candida*, *Miss Julie*, *Portia* and *Ella Rentheim* and is acknowledged as one of Britain's leading actresses. Two outstanding performances were in *Pick-Up Girl* and *Pin for the Peepshow*. Was the original *Picture Page* girl in pre-war television; since the war has played in Ibsen's *Rosmerholm* and *The Same Sky*. Now acting for television films under contract to Associated-Rediffusion Ltd.

STUDIOS AND SERVICES

Joined the B.B.C. in 1933 and worked in the North and Midland Regions as well as in London as a writer and producer of plays and feature radio productions, notably the scientific series *Look Ahead* and *The Lunar Society of the Air*. Transferred to television in 1953, as Organizer for the Documentary department until its dissolution in 1955. Now with B.B.C. Television Women's Programmes department.

Pre-war designer for film and theatre but specialized in exhibition design, having designed all B.B.C. Exhibition stands from 1933. Was with Ministry of Information's Exhibition Department during the war, designing sundry exhibitions for the Army, but returned to free-lance work in 1945. Chief co-ordinating designer for the Festival of Britain Travelling Exhibition, 1951. Joined the B.B.C. Television Service in 1953 as Head of Design.

After wide experience as resident designer for theatre stock companies in the United States, joined N.B.C. in 1944 as studio artist. Designed sets, made models and other studio artwork for experimental television, later becoming art director and then manager of production facilities. Since 1952 has concentrated on independent designing for television and is art director to Talent Associates Ltd., New York. Author of *Operation Backstage, Designing for TV* and *Staging TV Programs and Commercials*.

Joined B.B.C. Television in 1946 and worked mainly on cameras, but also had experience in vision control and sound floor operation. Has been Lighting Supervisor for seven years on many productions but notably *Dial M for Murder, Rose Without a Thorn, Passionate*

Pilgrim, Peer Gynt, The Sleeping Princess, The Eye of the Gypsy and *Return to Living.* Now with Associated-Rediffusion Ltd.

Joined B.B.C. Television in 1938, returning to it after war service in 1946. Has held various technical posts in television studio productions, specializing for past six years in sound. Now Assistant Head of Technical Operations, B.B.C. Television.

Had early photographic and radio experience and worked with the Baird Television Company in 1929, taking part in the first low definition transmission by the B.B.C., which he joined in 1932. Specialized since in lighting, experimental techniques, telerecording processes and many other aspects of television. Has contributed much to B.B.C. television technical development. Now in charge of Special Effects for B.B.C. Television.

THE SCOPE OF TELEVISION

In radio since 1939, and television since 1944, Dr. Cassirer was television news-editor for C.B.S., New York, until 1949, after which he wrote and produced many documentary and public affairs programmes, including C.B.S. colour television and current affairs quiz *It's News to Me.* Since 1952 he has been Head of Unesco's television section in Paris and is author, for that United Nations agency, of *Television: A World Survey* (1953), *Supplement* (1955).

Entered journalism in 1937 and after war service became film and theatre critic of the *Brighton Evening Argus*, Brighton being a try-out place for London theatrical productions. Joined the *Daily Mail* in 1950, becoming its television and radio critic in 1952. Regarded as one of the most progressive and best-informed television critics in Britain.

A leading British public relations expert, he has been closely concerned with the development of commercial television in the United Kingdom from its earliest stages. Companies with which he is associated have been responsible for the presentation of commercials for more than twenty leading British advertisers.

Has written and produced more American television commercials than any other man, having previously had wide journalistic, radio, theatre and advertising experience. Author of *The TV Commercial,* he is now Vice-President in charge of radio and television for McCann, Erickson Inc., New York. His new book, *TV Production Handbook,* appears in 1956.

INTRODUCTION

TELEVISION—you can welcome it, you can deplore it but you can't ignore it without being out-of-step with the majority of your friends, neighbours and crowds in the street. Television is no longer a luxury; to many people it is a necessity.

To some people it is the cheapest form of entertainment to hand, to others it is a thief of time needed for more worthwhile things. To others still, it is an up-to-the-split-second way of keeping abreast with current events, or a means of passively killing time, or a stimulus to go do things yourself, or an instrument of mass-hypnotism destroying the arts of reading and writing, or a welding-force among what (Carl Sandberg reminds us) Lincoln called the Family of Man.

Despite all this, maybe because of it, television can now capture an audience of up to at least 12 million people in the United Kingdom for its best programmes in a popular sense. For the exceptional event, such as the Coronation of 1953, it gets on for twice that number. The B.B.C.'s estimate of its average viewing audience in Britain is 5½ million persons (December, 1955). Over 5 million licences have been sold; 5 million wire-frames thrusting up from Subtopia and beyond. In the United States, television is as essential a part of the home as the automobile or the ice-box. Nearly 40 million American homes have television sets. Unesco informs us that 15 nations now have television in public operation, each with more than 50,000 receivers in their country. Many more countries have television round-the-corner. Its strides know no check.

Much abuse of television has been aimed at the medium instead of at the people who put on its programmes, or who pay for its programmes to be put on. There is nothing wrong with the medium itself except perhaps the smallness of its screen when compared with that of the cinema; but whose living-room is big enough these days for a full-size movie-screen? Its lack of detail and definition, this will disappear just as film stock has improved. The progress made in technical developments since the war has been prodigious. The technical resources both video and sound available to a producer at the B.B.C.'s present temporary London studios are far ahead of the use sometimes made of them.

Television is also a very expensive medium.

What is really important about television, over and above its obvious asset of immediacy, is its access to people in their own homes. Here its social influence is still at a primitive stage of measurement. Of first importance to the television producer is the realization that the viewing audience is different from other audiences. It is potentially vast in total, but actually small in audience per receiving set. An average cinema audience in Britain consists of 750 persons sitting closely together in rows facing the screen. Laughter by a handful of them can set the full audience laughing. Mass-instinct is very strong. An average television audience is probably two or three persons sitting informally in familiar home surroundings with every possibility of concentration being interrupted. To go to the cinema necessitates a journey of some kind, possibly a queue, and payment for seats. To view television necessitates the turning of a knob, after you've bought your set, that is, and in some countries paid your licence-fee.

This vast difference in what may be called " audience receptivity " must condition the programme content and presentation technique of television. We all know that television is for the most part an intimate medium. It is like looking through a telescope the wrong way round. In the intimacy of the home, sincerity of intention by performer and producer can far outstrip spectacle and sensationalism. *Quo Vadis?* belongs to the cinema. The cabaret act, the Little Theatre play,

10

the personal performance, belong to television—especially the projection of personality. Let every television producer and writer recall the words of Maeterlinck: " It is in a small room, round the table, close to the fire, that the joys and sorrows of mankind are decided."[1]

Television, some say, may corrupt and disrupt family life but, say others, it may also prove to be an immense factor in social education, not only influencing opinions but conditioning behaviour. In the immediate post-war years, television in Britain was an entertainment for the "better-off." Today, exactly the opposite is true. It is important to realize that a big proportion of viewers consists of people who seldom read a book or go to the theatre. Their social attitude until recently has largely been shaped by the movies, mainly American ones, and to a certain extent by the radio. And, of course, by the more sensational of the daily newspapers. There is, agreed, a danger of mass-hypnosis by this new medium and the uniformity of its content. On the other hand, those who predicted by American precedent that television would sway votes at the last General Election in Britain appear to have been mistaken. Maybe that denotes a difference between the mass-mind and individualism? There are signs that British viewers do select their programmes (after the novelty of the set has worn off) and they are likely to do so more now there is an alternative service. The fact that programme content and production particulars are published in advance is an inducement to select. The service performed by the *Radio Times*, with its 8,800,000 circulation, in Britain is not to be under-estimated. No such detailed public guide exists for any other form of mass-entertainment.

Television could, if developed for the common good, raise immeasurably the thinking, the conduct, the very way of living of the world's people, let alone of a nation. Such views are held apparently by the Independent Television Authority, to judge by its first annual report, but regrettably they do not appear to be supported by the programme contractors it licenses —as yet. The tremendous social implications of television emerge, I think, from some of the contributions to this book. Dr. Henry Cassirer, for example, makes an important point in

[1] *I am indebted to Michael Orrom and Raymond Williams' book* Preface to Film (*Film Drama, 1954*) *for this quotation made in 1889.*

saying that the spread of world television has not been confined to those countries with a high standard of living or a well-developed industrial economy, and cites Cuba and the Philippines. Television may well prove an influential factor, like atomic energy, in the social betterment of what are called the under-developed countries. No doubt the United Nations and its Specialized Agencies have this well in mind.

One big danger of television, I admit, is its insatiable demands on talent. The constant need for fresh programme material, day after day, night after night, is both terrifying and conducive to the lowering of standards. True, there are whole new worlds to be explored by television's roving cameras, a whole new field of talent to be discovered in regional areas, but the very speed which daily programming dictates can too easily lead to slipshod thinking and undigested viewpoints. (In my own *genre*, I have noted how quickly the considered documentary approach can degenerate into superficial reporting.) Technically, this matters less than the decadence of the creative thought from which the programme is born. Technically, television gets away with murder in the name of " actuality " but the mere *presentation* of actuality itself is not in itself creative. This is something on which both the academic minds of the B.B.C. and the showmen of commercial television might well reflect—when they have time.

It could be that we have reached a position where technocracy streaks electronically ahead, outstripping the process of human creative thought. Maybe we are already in an era where the technical skills of distribution machinery for mass-entertainment have become too proficient for the available talent to make the creative product for transmission? Compare a motion picture, which perhaps takes six months to plan and complete (a relatively short period) and then has a world distribution life of at least three to five years, with a television show that takes a few weeks to plan (if that), a few days or hours to rehearse and produce and a distribution life limited to an hour or so at the most—unless recorded on celluloid. Simultaneous viewing by vast audiences may outstrip the supply of potential creative talent for production—unless repeat performance is acceptable. Technological efficiency is swallowing human creative effort at a greater rate than it can be regenerated. Television already has at hand plenty of producers with the

12

bare "know-how" of how to put a "live" show on the air, but the show will not live creatively for the future. But is television at all concerned with the future? Its current aim is to satisfy the casual needs of the moment. Hence the phrase heard in television studios—" Anything goes."

The danger of this immediacy in television is very real. It can be tempting to think that because a programme is going out tonight it will be forgotten tomorrow. To present a programme simultaneously to 10 million people at one performance is surely no less important or responsible than showing it to them at hundreds of separate performances over a stretch of months? The ephemeral nature of television is one of its major problems if we are to consider it in all seriousness as a creative medium.

The secondary use of television to show film in place of "live" material may be denigrated by some of television's exponents and by some of its critics, but the mere fact that a programme is being recorded, can be re-seen and re-used, is in itself stimulating to more careful first-thought. Film is not a substitute for "live" and immediate television; it is a different but wholly legitimate use of the medium's machinery for reproduction, just as is radio's use of recordings. And film can give time for thought, for research, for reflection and careful consideration of content and argument. It is possible that the attitude of so many television-trained people, especially in the B.B.C., towards film is not so much antipathy against celluloid itself as envy of the professional skill already attained by film people which television in its infancy has yet to acquire. Fortunately the economics of television are such that the sale of programmes outside their country of origin will become increasingly necessary to recoup production outlay, which must mean a greater use of recorded programmes with all the advantages it carries; recordings, that is, made both at the time of "live" transmission off-the-tube (if technically improved in quality) and films made primarily for television distribution.

Frequency of performance and the fleeting life of that performance, these are two of the many problems thrown up by the inherent nature of television that must be tackled right away if the medium is to be a social and creative contributor to the common good. If they are excused on the grounds that television is just entertainment, showmanship, "escape from the realities of life," we shall be abusing what surely is the most powerful means of contact between man and man yet invented.

Is television an art in itself? None of the electro-mechanical media—film, radio or television—are in themselves an art. They are only instruments of infinite complexity to be creatively used. Television has so far shone by its basic capability to "see at a distance," to reproduce actuality "as it happens." There is nothing especially *creative* about this. The Coronation of Queen Elizabeth, a milestone in television technical history, was not produced, directed, written, designed or staged by the B.B.C. Television Service although a brilliantly successful transmission was made of what took place in front of its cameras. The producer's skill lay in the placing of his cameras and microphones and his decisions when to use each of them in turn when on the air, as will be seen in Mr. Peter Dimmock's fascinating piece in this book. But I do not think that Mr. Dimmock would claim that there was anything creative about the achievement any more than the captain of a stratocruiser would claim to be a creative artist each time he flies his aircraft safely across the Atlantic. There is today an increasing tendency to mistake operational technical skill for creative artistry.

To date I have seen nothing on the television screen to suggest that the medium itself has greater technical facility than the film, except this blessed quality of immediacy. But immediacy itself denies all too often a fundamental requisite of the artist—the right to select in contemplation. Television's immediacy is an added and very exciting attribute to the technique of reporting, but reporting (or recording) is not a creative art. Failure by the B.B.C. to recognize this distinction perhaps explains its confusion between Talks and Documentary programmes? Even in its own journal, *The Listener*, under a column headed "Documentary," most space is given to discussing Talks and Outside Broadcasts because, I suppose, they too deal with "real" material.

As Miss Joan Miller remarks in her contribution about acting, television has still to be used by a Griffith, or, to be in the present, by a De Sica or a Max Ophuls or a Clouzot. Nothing has yet been realized in television of the quality and significance of a *Bicycle Thieves* or a *Potemkin* or a *Song of Ceylon*. Maybe this is no fault of the medium but a failure of its promoters and controllers to employ such artists. A De

14

Sica handling outside-broadcast cameras, an Ophuls given the flexibility of the television medium, this could be something if the time was there for thought and experiment. Perhaps it is significant that very few, if any, top-flight film-makers have so far shown much interest in producing for this medium?

Television's greatest problem for all artists is, I repeat, paradoxically enough in its inherent quality of immediacy. If those who control the medium, be they advertisers or public servants, can make available the minimum requirements of the artists, then something creatively exciting might happen. The advertising sponsors of the medium and those who serve their needs mostly have a quick-sale motive to pursue; the B.B.C. has not. Now that there is an alternative television service in Britain, let us hope that the B.B.C. will commission much more experimental work than it has so far done. Let the Corporation now take some of the risks that it was not ready to take when it was the sole provider.

*   *   *   *

Britain is the first country in the world to have both television as a public service paid for by the licence-fees of viewers and television provided by commercial interests for advertising purposes combined with the possibility of limited Government funds. The experiment is remarkable to watch. No viewer disputes the need for an alternative service to that put out by the B.B.C., but there must be many who are still puzzled as to why the B.B.C. itself should not have been permitted to supply the alternative, which indeed it intends doing in the not-so-distant future. And no one pursued the proposal put forward in the correspondence columns of *The Times* at the peak of the violent discussions for combining public service television with a system of sponsorship, in the same way that the British documentary film has been financed over the years.

So be it, we have now our Independent Television Authority with a front almost as urbane as the B.B.C. itself. What shape, size and quality British commercial television will be in a year's time is anyone's guess right now. At present it is feeling its way with only one station working, relying on the obvious and taking care not to be " serious." Its main disappointment, after only some three months' transmission, is that it has been too much like the B.B.C. and has so far failed to produce television-wise a single new idea.

We have been told, however, that the providers of commercial television have already learned that it is not their job to improve the minds of the public. Their job, they say, is to attract the largest number of viewers to see the advertisements in between programmes, which hardly squares with the views of the Director-General of the Independent Television Authority when he said that television programmes " ought to express the coherent policy and outlook of a group of people conscious that what they have in their hands is a social responsibility, a life-charging force for the direction of which they are responsible."[1] One top-executive of British commercial television has been quoted as saying: "From now on what the public wants, it's going to get," while another has gone on the record with: " The question you have to ask yourself is this: ' How low is the public taste?' and the answer is this: ' As low as you force it. You can never force it up.' "[2] That, of course, is a most flagrant denial of the whole process of education, and by implication a proposal that the mass-public should be kept where it belongs. Back to illiteracy and ignorance!

In this crazy stampede to " give the public what it wants " there is already grave danger that television's long-term social importance and significance may be trodden underfoot. It is an ill-considered statement to boast that one knows " what the public wants " even if viewer research figures appear to confirm one's views. It is an alibi for ignoring the responsibility of power and power indeed the executives and programme-controllers of television possess. If it is a fact that research enquiry reveals that in Britain a moron-level of television programme content is demanded, then it is difficult to equate this finding with the fact that such a seriously handled film as The Dambusters, with few of the conventional entertainment ingredients as understood by the film trade, headed the list of British box-office successes last year. Or are we to believe that one level of criticism should be applied to commercial films and another—if indeed it is a level at all—to television viewing?

In summing-up television progress at the end of 1955, I note

[1] The Coming of Independent Television, published by the Independent Television Authority, London, 1955.
[2] Picture Post, December 3, 1955.

that our responsible critics are more than a little disturbed by the thought that so poor is most television programme quality that it is now impracticable to judge it by the critical standards applied to literature, music, theatre, radio or the cinema. To quote Mr. Peter Black: " The most dismaying reflection on the current popularity ratings of television programmes is that they are so bad that they must be true. Even if it wanted to, no organization could invent figures that put television and its audience in a more discreditable light. The worst of the list of the Top Ten published yesterday is that you can run your eye down it and up again without encountering a single programme that represents the balanced television which everybody—politicians and bishops, B.B.C. and independent television—knows to be the only kind that can keep the audience from turning into a nation of passive morons."[1] Much of what does go out today over both our television services is meretricious and trivial, characteristic of the Admass period in which we exist, as Mr. Priestley has it, and in keeping with the anti-cultural trend which is today the fashion in some circles. If it were not for the spotlight of the national press beamed fiercely on to television, most of it would go unremarked for ever—one hopes! The unwarranted amount of space given to television by our newspapers (alleged to be short of newsprint!) is symptomatic of our times.

*　　　　*　　　　*　　　　*

The B.B.C. is committed by its charter to inform, educate and entertain. Commercial television—despite the words of Sir Robert Fraser—is committed to nothing beyond observing the normal disciplines of public behaviour and certain restrictions on what products it can publicize—except that it has to satisfy its advertisers that it can catch a big audience. One notes already that the B.B.C. and commercial television are quarrelling about the size of their respective audience coverage. The future of commercial television in this country will be a severe test of industrial and advertising good-sense as well as of the integrity of the Independent Television Authority, a test for which we have been let in by a Government which, in my opinion, should never have allowed television as a part of national life to become a matter of party politics.

[1] Daily Mail, *December 29, 1955.*

B.B.C. Radio has in thirty-three years become a professional undertaking with creative, technical and cultural standards of its own devising. B.B.C. Television is still very young. It has grown up fast. It has had to venture out into the zoo-world of show-business more widely than has radio. It has also had to learn by short-cut the business of film-making at the same time as discovering television itself. It was inevitable that some amateurism should characterize its activity. As a Corporation financed out of public funds and answerable to Parliament through the Postmaster General, the B.B.C. has modelled its administration on the Civil Service although not of it. B.B.C. Television has a fine record in engineering; its weakness to date has been its failure to devise administration machinery flexible enough to accommodate the needs of the creative artist—be he writer, producer or director—to allow for the resilience, the temperament or that occasional streak of lunacy that so often go with creative activity. Administrative minds prefer the foreseeable, the orthodox, the kind of respectable talent that can be evaluated and filed at an annual interview.

On the other hand, the B.B.C. has—with its restricted financial resources—explored television with a public school heartiness and a boyish sense of adventure, especially in the field of Outside Broadcasts. Its Drama, too, has had its successes, but perhaps has sometimes been expected to do too much with too few resources. Its Documentary department, now disbanded, achieved programmes of social importance that consistently won warm public response and more often than not critical praise from those who mattered. It is good that the B.B.C. has not dropped programmes of this kind altogether and that Mr. Norman Swallow's two series, *Special Enquiry* and *The World is Ours*, still continue. It has pioneered with its Children's department and some of its personality talks have been notable. B.B.C. Television has, in all, much of which to be proud. It is not fighting its battle with commercial television in the field of talent alone. Equally important is its need to devise machinery which permits that talent full scope to flourish.

In the United States, where it has been developed almost wholly on an advertisement-sponsored basis, television has partly revolutionized the political, social and industrial life of the nation. It has become a billion dollar industry in the biggest way. The estimated advertising revenue for last year

18

was said to be set at 1,000 million dollars. But this very bigness contains within it the seeds of problems. Coast-to-coast television is so regular and reliable that it comes as a shock to realize how many areas of that vast country are still out of range of a television service. The B.B.C., we should remember, as a public service not concerned with consumer markets, aims to cover virtually the entire United Kingdom with a television service and has very nearly done so. In New York, programmes are costing astronomical figures; 100,000 dollars is not exceptional for a top-line show, without reckoning the cost of air-time. It is for this reason, and because there is a tendency for sponsors to work collaboratively, that " controversial " programmes are avoided. Ed. Murrow in his *Person to Person* and *See It Now* is an exception. On the other hand, I found there last year a greater interest in public affairs programmes both among stations and the press. It is possible, for example, for Mr. Henry Salomon to have his own documentary unit under the ægis of the National Broadcasting Company; his *Victory at Sea* series and *Three-Two-One-Zero* programme will be long remembered. And Mr. Alistair Cooke still runs his culture-guide *Omnibus*, which owed its initiation to the Ford Foundation.

After a bitter initial fight, Hollywood is coming to terms with its competitor and may even move in on the field in a big way. Hundreds upon hundreds of short television films have been made by the smaller companies there in the past few years (we are seeing all too many of them here today), but now the major companies are interested. Subscription television, disliked by the networks and advertisers because viewers may become more selective if they have to pay to see programmes, can greatly interest Hollywood. It conjures up a dream in which the complete production costs of a film could be recouped by a single television transmission with viewers paying in their homes by coin-box or by telephone account. Unlike the structure in this country, American film production is divorced from exhibition. If producers could by-pass exhibitors by taking their films direct into the home, where then would stand the exhibitor? He has only his wide-screen to protect him.

Round the corner, too, is colour television, already being transmitted to a restricted few because of the set expense. Even more important, the biggest revolution of all, is video

19

tape-recording by which pictures as well as sounds can be recorded on magnetic tape. Away with film and celluloid, processing and all those time-wasters! Video-tape, they say, can be played back almost immediately. It can be wired, they say, from place to place. Once again, it is in the service of speed and immediacy, slashing the time for thought and skill. None the less, it will be with us to be used, like the cinema's wide-screen which no creative artist asked for. Technocracy streaks ahead irrespective of how its discoveries and gifts are put to work. Television is here before more than a handful of men have learned how to use the motion picture properly. Perhaps television will, by cutting out the middle-man, by piping its product direct to the viewer, find more opportunity for the creative artist who has been so frustrated in the cinema? Perhaps we may see ahead the day when, by providing the lowest possible kind of entertainment, television will allow the film to grow to adulthood?

* * * *

Television is, verily, " in the making "—every minute, hour, night and day. Thus the contributions that make up this book have been selected from two points of view. Some deal with television in what may be called a general way, such as Dr. Cassirer's survey of its world-growth and possible significance to peoples in many countries. Others—the majority—take various fields of activity in television production. Here the expert tells of his own work and its problems, indicating how such work might appeal to others and what are the qualifications needed. In such an interdependent medium as television, with its many skills and departments and where teamwork is essential, with its associations with the theatre and the film, it is inevitable that some of our contributors overlap into each other's field. Only in this way could an overall survey of the complexities of television production be made. It should be pointed out, too, that some contributors deal with their sub ject only as it is practised at the B.B.C. and, since until very recently that body has been the only television service in the United Kingdom, a large proportion are, or have been, B.B.C. people.

There may be what at first sight appear to be omissions. No separate section, for example, deals with film and television but several contributors make reference to the use of film in television. B.B.C. Television has made few films itself. It does, however, acquire films from outside sources where and when it can rent them, but this does not call for comment here. Audience research is another subject that in general has been considered as outside our scope, although it crops up inevitably in Mr. John Metcalf's piece about television as an advertising medium, and elsewhere. And so, section by section, the reader can, I hope, pattern together a composite picture of what television production means, what are its possibilities and what is the inexhaustible power that the television exponent has in his hands. The opening of commercial television in Britain has meant greater demands on talent of all kinds—producers, writers, designers, cameramen, actors, technicians of many skills—and to those coming fresh into television this book may serve as a useful source of information, possibly even inspiration.

The Glossary of Television and Film Terms is, as far as I am aware, the most complete to be published in this country. Of film glossaries alone there are many but few are good. Numerous television glossaries are published in the United States, with an ever-increasing coinage of slang-terms which differ from station to station across that vast country, but of those consulted few are accurate. I am grateful, therefore, to Mr. Harry McMahan, who also contributes to this book, for giving me access to the advance proof of his *TV Today*; and also to the B.B.C. for its generous permission to draw from its *Glossary of Broadcasting Terms* (1941) and subsequent supplements prepared for its own internal use. My thanks also go to Mr. Ian Atkins, the experienced drama producer of the B.B.C., who in recent months has been allocated to special duties that brought him into close touch with all sides of television, including a visit to the United States, for advice in preparing the Glossary; and to Mr. Ken Cameron, for many years senior sound-recordist at the Crown Film Unit and now with Messrs. Anvil Films, both for his advice and for permission to use some sound-recording definitions from the glossary of his own book, *Sound and the Documentary Film* (Pitman, 1947). Acknowledgement is also made to the B.B.C. for providing the material on which the plans and lay-outs in this book have been based.

All the contributors to this book are very busy people; they work in or with television. I thank them for their contributions and ask their pardon for having made their lives a misery until I had prised their manuscripts from them. Finally, my thanks to Miss Moyna Kitchin, my secretary while I had the privilege to head the B.B.C.-Television Documentary department, for her help in preparing the texts for the press.

*   *   *   *

Brought up on the movies, from the red-plush curtain and wooden tip-up seat to the elephantiasis antics of today, it might be thought that I am biased against television. That is not so: I respect its dynamic immediacy and I envy its easy access to vast audiences. I accept it as an inevitable part of our life and hope to see it used for each and all of its many purposes. If I did not see it this way, I should not have spent two years working in it with, I hope, both a sense of responsibility and a sense of humour. But, as a last thought, no one need fear that I shall one day write a *TV Till Now*.

Let the experts now have their say.

P. R.

January, 1956.

PROGRAMMES
AND PRODUCERS

THE TELEVISION DRAMA

J. ROYSTON MORLEY

TELEVISION may be defined as a method of visual and aural communication by which moving or still pictures, accompanied by appropriate sound, are received at a point remote from the place of their origination. The production of television programmes is a method of publication. The B.B.C.'s television programmes are intended to instruct, inform and entertain, each programme when possible combining the three requirements.

In the pre-war Television Service, the maximum effort was put into the production of drama programmes, and it is fair to say that here were evolved the techniques which were later copied by producers of other types of programmes. And even now, after nineteen years, the B.B.C. Sunday night play is always an important event in a week's viewing.

A play, whether presented to an audience in the theatre, in a cinema, or on a television screen, is basically a method of conveying ideas, expressed in words and spoken by people. For years it has been fashionable in television and film circles to talk at length about something called " a visual medium," to expatiate on the necessity of carrying on the story " visually," and to illustrate a doubtful premise by moving back to the silent film or on to the possible excitements resulting from setting-up a television camera to watch the crowds at Piccadilly Circus, or from allowing it to photograph the unrestrained performances of animals. This attitude arises partly from an over-enthusiasm which tries to pretend that television is more important than it is, and partly from a confusion between programmes which deal with life as " it is lived "—and television lets us see it as it is lived—and programmes which gain their interest from art and not from life.

Drama is fiction, and if it is successful, its success is an artistic success. In other words, television drama is art, and it will succeed or fail by the ideas it puts forward, as well as by the skill with which the dramatic situations are developed and the way in which the actors play their parts.

In all serious drama, words cannot be neglected. It is true that in the film the writer may be regarded as an amateur, and there are always plenty of so-called "script-doctors," experts in the craft of camera-angles and editing, who will pretend to tell the author how to carry on his story in "visuals." Nine times out of ten, all they do is to reduce a thing of subtlety to a formula—and a pretty dull formula, too—and to make all films they touch look like a copy of a copy. This does not, of course, mean that an author cannot get good advice from the members of a script department—least of all in television—but it must always be remembered that it is advice to be taken or left at the writer's discretion. There is no mystique about writing for television any more than there is about writing for the theatre or for the cinema screen. What is important is the realization that the author is the *sine qua non*, and that in the final event a dramatic programme will stand or fall by the actual construction and writing of the drama, and by the importance of the idea behind it. Brilliant acting and production and brilliance of technique cannot make bricks without straw.

This realization is the starting point for the television drama producer. It applies equally to tragedy, comedy, farce, thrillers and serials. In a conveyor-belt business like modern television this is a hard fact to recognize and harder to accept. With a drama output of something near 150 plays a year, chances must be and are taken. But any organization which seeks to put the author in a secondary place will head for desperate troubles; the author seeking to express himself in television terms has enough of his own troubles in any case.

One of these is a lack of discipline in what is still a new medium. Our best dramatic writing and production in Britain is to be found in the theatre, where difficulties and limitations are realized and accepted. The theatre author knows that managers require intervals, that time must be allowed for scenery to be changed, that actors need intervals (or time off the stage)

26

to alter costume or make-up. But in television many of these difficulties—or disciplines as I prefer to call them—do not exist. The television producer can allow the author to move from set to set—from the deck of the *Queen Mary* to the sitting-room of the third officer's home—filmed sequences can be inserted at will, and time can be played with as easily as location. This can make for slipshod construction. It can allow the story-line to get tangled in a mass of visual changes, destroy characterization, and not give the characters enough words to permit real artistic development.

This last has been the destruction of many hopeful films. Things happen, the characters react, more things happen, the characters react again. At the end, they are just as they were at the start. We feel, perhaps, "Alan Ladd certainly went through a lot, he experienced quite a bit, but in character he seems completely unaltered." This should never be the case, whether we are watching *King Lear* in the theatre, *Citizen Kane* in the cinema, or Sam Palmer in *The Final Test* on television. The television drama producer, therefore, should not discourage the author from using words in the dramatic sense, and must find a way of using his visuals to enrich the words and so to heighten the impact of the play.

Producing for television is a difficult and complex operation. Nine-tenths of what is seen on the screen in a play is in "live" action. Editing and second thoughts are not possible. It is as if the film director were asked to make a ninety-minute feature film in one "take" and to edit the film at the same time. Live action television means shooting in sequence and putting the responsibility for the individual performance upon the individual actor once the show is running. Details of playing and interpretation are guided by the producer in rehearsal, but in television, "on the night," the actor gives his own performance. The producer's task then is to ensure that the visuals are handled efficiently, artistically and with dramatic effect.

This is achieved by very careful and detailed planning and results from a visual imagination on the producer's part during the rehearsal period. Imagination is important because the play does not move into the studio until the day before transmission. The two or three weeks of rehearsal take place in a large room, the sets exist only as chalk-marks on the floor showing where doors and windows and staircases are going to

27

be, and oak tables and metal tubular chairs stand for marble-topped desks and imperial thrones. Somehow the producer must help the actors to visualize these things so that they will find them in the studio without a sense of surprise. " Ah," says the actor seeing perhaps a four-poster bed in the studio, " I imagined it would be like that."

The position of the cameras and the sound-boom carrying the microphone must be planned in advance, moments to change shot by cutting or dissolving from camera to camera arranged, effects considered and ordered, back-projection slides photographed and all the multitude of aids to production chosen.

In the studio, the producer controls his play as it goes out over the air. The camera-operators, the sound-engineers and the stage management on the studio floor wear headphones connected to a microphone in the control-room where the producer sits. For in television the producer works away from the studio floor. He sees before him a number of television screens—one for each camera he is using—and a transmission screen showing the picture from whatever camera is on the air—i.e., the one giving a picture which the audience is also seeing. In drama productions four cameras are normally used, tracking quite freely in the studio, and often moving from one setting to another as the action of the play demands.

Cutting from camera to camera is carried out by the vision-mixer sitting beside the producer. A shooting-script indicates where the shot is to be changed and how, but most producers tell the vision-mixer the exact moment to make the change. Similarly, the producer briefs the sound-mixer of the likely change from one microphone to another and warns the microphone operators on the studio floor when he intends going from close-up to long-shot, so that the microphone itself will not appear in picture. Difficulties—and there are always many—are ironed out in the first day of studio rehearsal, compromises are made and improvements tried. But once the play moves from rehearsal-room to studio the emphasis is upon techniques. It is too late to try and alter acting performances. This is a great disadvantage for the television producer; but so long as there are not enough television studios to handle a growing output the producer must put up with this. Ideally a week on the studio floor is needed to mount a major play.

Prior to the actual rehearsal period, the television producer

28

HAROLD CLAYTON'S PRODUCTION OF "ROMEO AND JULIET"
FOR B.B.C. TELEVISION, MAY 22, 1955

Pages 30 and 31. *The studio floor with sets erected but no camera positions as yet indicated.*

Key to Numbers:

First Set: Balcony Scene.
    1. Dressing-room for artiste's quick-change, etc.
    2. The Balcony.
    3. Stand microphone (fixed).
    4. Six-foot high Wall.
    6. Well made of plaster.
    7. Grass made of matting.
    8. Tree in Juliet's Garden.
    9. Exterior Garden Wall and Lane.

Second Set: Friar Lawrence's Cell.
    10. The Cell.
    11. Tybalt's Catafalque (on rollers).
    12. Backcloth: vista of Verona.
    13. A Street: seen in perspective.
    14. Apothecary's Door.

Third Set: Juliet's Bedroom and Ante-chamber.
    1. Dressing-room for artiste's quick-change, etc.
    2. Balcony.
    15. Drapes on movable arm.
    16. Juliet's Bedroom.
    17. Drapes on runner.
    18. Juliet's Ante-room.
    19. A Column (one of four) in position for Ball scene.

Fourth Set: 20. Capulet's Hall.

Fifth Set: 21. Passage and Door leading to the Tomb (on rostrum).
    22. Interior of the Tomb and Catafalque (see 11).

Sixth Set: 23. A Fountain (practical) for Street scene.
    24. Off-stage steps and artiste's dressing-room.

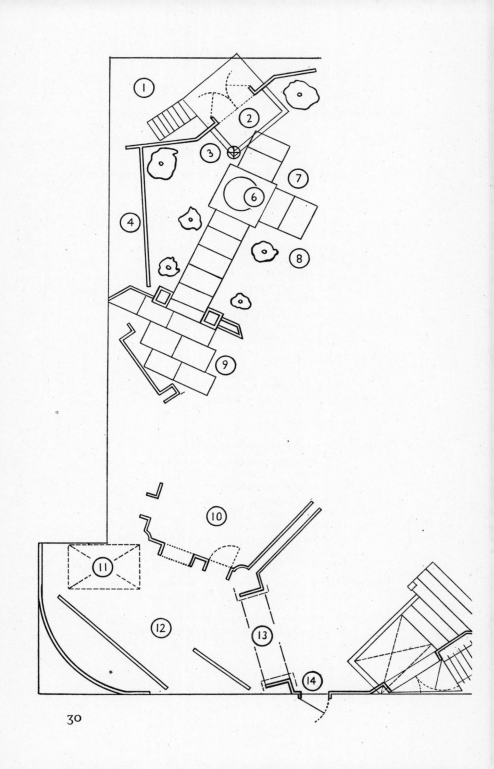

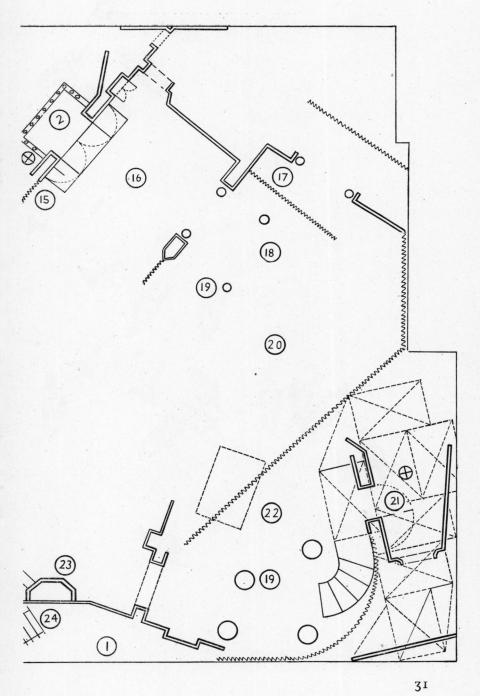

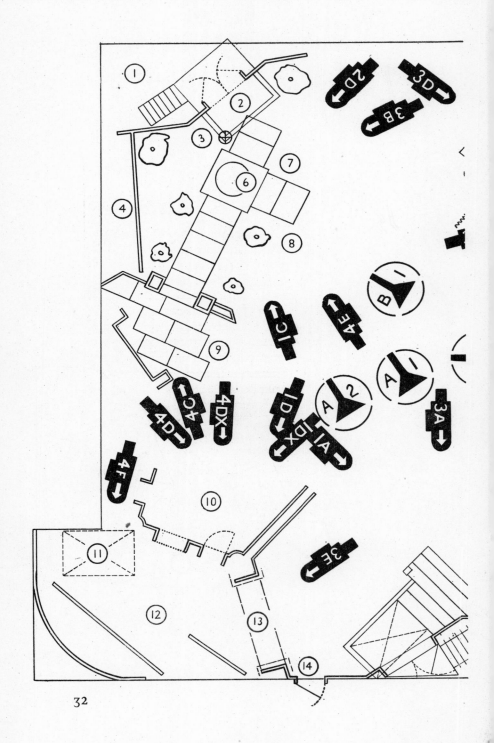

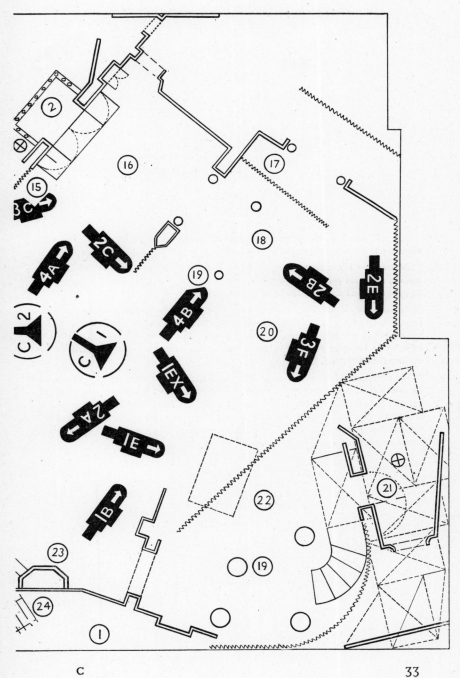

Pages 32 and 33. The same studio floor as shown on pages 30 and 31 but with camera and microphone positions indicated.

Although in a drama production of this kind both cameras and microphones are mobile, they have certain basic positions from which they operate. Four cameras are to be used and their movements can be traced thus:

Camera One's opening set-up is marked I A. When the Producer has finished using it from this position and has changed to another camera, Camera One is moved to its second set-up marked I B, and so on to I C and I D. The move from I D to I DX is effected by swinging part of the camera-dolly to a different angle without actually moving the dolly itself.

The microphone booms need to be less mobile than the cameras, but they also must be moved to accommodate the action of the artistes. Boom A, for example, starts in position indicated at A I and then is moved to A 2: C I moves to C 2, and so on. It should be pointed out that the microphones themselves are suspended from long, telescopic boom-arms and can thus be swung into many positions to follow the action without their basic set-up being changed.

has been responsible for helping to find (or commission) a suitable play for production. He has estimated likely costs, including the designing and building of settings, of cast, of an orchestra (if he is using one), of any specially shot or hired film he wishes to use, and so on. It is also his responsibility to select the most suitable available actors and to ask a booking-section to arrange their fees within his budget.

The producer will also spend time with his designer. Together the two will evolve ground-plans and sketches, working much in the same way as they would in the theatre or cinema. This is followed by early meetings with the sound and vision technicians who are going to work on the programme so that snags may be spotted in advance. Lighting is one of the greatest problems because the lighting-supervisor must light for continuous action. He must offer a kind of lighting which will cover long-shots and close-ups on the same set with the minimum of readjustment while the play is actually being transmitted. The careful producer tries to have a good idea of where his close-ups are coming well in advance so that he can tell his lighting-supervisor in the planning stage and difficulties can be thrashed out early.

In just the same way, sound sources must be considered with the sound-mixer; a happy compromise between sound and lighting is vital. Any impasse between the two would be fatal to the play, and the producer has to lead his team rather than drive it.

Once the play is in the studio, a floor-manager, with his assistants, takes over the responsibility for carrying out the producer's orders—and intentions—on the studio floor. Like his colleagues he listens to the producer by headphones. The good producer tries to keep his floor-manager aware all the time of what he is trying to do so that the meaning behind his orders is clear.

Now that television programmes are frequently recorded off the live transmission, the drama producer has other worries. For a start, telerecording clips the frame of the picture both vertically and horizontally, and it is necessary to remember this when lining-up shots. And the question of retakes has to be kept in mind. These may result from technical trouble during transmission, or from " fluffing " of lines by actors. On the other hand, the possession of the right to record is vitally

35

important to both television and the producer. The latter can for the first time watch one of his productions in peace and quiet, away from the turmoil of the control-room, and attempt to assess his mistakes.

Filmed sequences, shot in advance of the live transmission and cut in at the right time during the course of the play, add further complications. Most of these tend to be exteriors, but, when interiors are used, great care is needed to match the lighting of the filmed sequence with the lighting to be expected in the same set in the studio. The producer must also be careful that the tempo of cutting in the filmed sequence matches the tempo of cutting he expects to use in the live action. Overall, television cutting is much slower than that normally used in the cinema, partly because the screen is smaller and partly because of the importance in drama of the words. It is also dangerous in prefilmed sequences to use many true reverse-angles because these are never obtainable in live television—although a skilful producer can often make an audience imagine that they are seeing a true reverse-angle.

The responsibilities of the television drama producer are great but the opportunities are equally great. As a new generation of creative writers grows up—people who cannot remember the time when there was no television set in the home —new and exciting writing for television will result. The medium will offer its own disciplines and the writer will accept them. Until that time, the drama producer's main trouble in Britain is lack of new writers, lack of rehearsal time in the studio and the absence of colour. In the next five or ten years we can hope these difficulties and handicaps will resolve themselves.

WRITING FOR TELEVISION

ARTHUR SWINSON

THE major problem facing any writer coming fresh to television is to understand what it is. Is it a new art medium or merely a new method of disseminating information? Is it simply an extension of radio, or is it just an inferior form of cinema? These are basic questions which require an answer. Before dealing with them, however, I would like to set down the three main problems which, in my belief, face any writer new to television. They are:

(1) The problem, already mentioned, of understanding the nature of the medium.

(2) The problems of time and space encountered in constructing the script.

(3) The problem of the lay-out of the script.

Now to deal with these in order. Perhaps the best way to start on the first is to compare television with other media and to plot its affinities and contrasts.

Like radio, it is broadcast to a mass-audience grouped in small numbers; it forms part of a daily service; it may be produced inside the studio, outside it, or both; and each programme is consumed in one performance, or a small number of performances. Like the film, it employs cameras and the action is seen through a lens; it is viewed on a screen; it employs simultaneously sound and vision; it employs grammatical devices such as the mix and fade. Like the theatre it is a live medium; its actors or actualities give a continuous performance.

Now for the points of divergence. Unlike radio, television must bow to the exacting demands of vision as well as sound. Unlike the film it is principally a live, as opposed to a recorded, medium—although this may change with time; its action has only relative mobility. Unlike the stage play, its action can move swiftly from set to set; it plays to small intimate groups of people at short range.

From this brief analysis it should be apparent that, although television draws characteristics from all these media, it can by no means be identified with any one of them. It has too many affinities with the film merely to be an extension of sound radio; it has too much of radio and the theatre merely to be an inferior form of cinema. It is a new and exciting medium in its own right. It is not even an alternative to the theatre or the cinema; it is rather a window on the world, a magic window through which can be seen passing all the sights and sounds and people of the day. Maurice Wiggin, the television critic, once called television " a periscope through which we can see how the world wags." This seems to me a definition it would be hard to better.

When I said that television was a live medium I was, of course, quite aware that it does employ both recorded sound (on disc or tape) and recorded vision (on film). Most plays and documentaries use linking filmed sequences and some types of programme (such as the famous *Special Enquiry* series) use a high proportion of film. When this happens television takes on temporarily the characteristics of a recorded medium, though its real nature remains the same. Being a live medium is the principal cause of what I have called the problems of time and space. These keep cropping up in various forms in every script and any writer who is determined to master television must develop a technique for dealing with them.

Let me give a simple example. In one scene a character called John Smith is drinking in a night club, dressed in a dinner jacket. In the next scene he is at his office next morning, dressed in a lounge suit. In a film, this would be quite straightforward. The action would be recorded shot by shot and edited together. In television, however, the position is quite different because shot follows shot and scene follows scene in real time. If John Smith has to change his costume the script must be constructed so as to give him enough time. Even if no change of costume is necessary, he must still be given time to walk from set to set, collecting any necessary " props " *en route.*

38

Occasionally the problem may be eased by the insertion of a linking film sequence but by no means every time. Within a scene the time factor still holds; if an actor has to lace up his boots, tie his tie, or even put on a car wheel, the actual time must be allowed. These actions cannot be telescoped, as in a film.

Closely allied with the problems of time are the problems of space and, indeed, they are often aspects of the same problem. Every set in the script has to be built and erected in the studio. Some sets can be managed by back-projection and other devices but, in general, all the sets demanded in the script must be erected side by side. From this it follows that their number will be limited by the available studio space; it is no use a writer asking for twenty-three sets, because he will never get them. He may get twelve; he is lucky to get more than eight.

This, considering the size of the larger studios, may seem an unnecessary curb on the writer, but there is a very good reason: the studio lay-out must take into account not only the disposition of the sets but the necessity of movement from set to set. The needs of the actors have already been touched on, but also there are the camera crews and their dollies, the microphone booms, the lighting men and a whole army of technicians. Unless they can keep up with the actors, the programme as a piece of television ceases to exist. The general rule is, therefore, that the more room there is for manœuvre, the faster the actors and the technicians can move.

At its best, television has only relative mobility and its action moves from set to set, or from set via film sequence to set. Within each set the action is usually pegged to a room, an office, a shop, or some other unit until it moves on to the next scene and is pegged there. It cannot (as in the film) move down corridors, along roads, and up hills or down precipices. For this reason the television scene is similar to the stage scene and the television script tends to consist of thirty to sixty such scenes, grouped into sequences and linked in the mounting rhythm of the action. I should add that this technique of writing was not invented by television writers nor borrowed direct from the cinema; it was developed by William Shakespeare. The number of sets and scenes employed in *Hamlet* or *Richard III* is very much the same as in a television script. If Shakespeare were alive today he would be our leading television writer. Certainly the present fashion for one-set plays would have driven him from the theatre.

How can these problems of time and space be reduced to a minimum? The only way, in my experience, is to work out a detailed construction of the script before a line of dialogue is written. In this should be included a synopsis of each scene and the characters involved in it, and the details of each set. If this is done systematically a good many snags will be apparent, and so may be dealt with, before it is too late. In fact, the construction should be worked on until it is near perfect because any faults that remain will show up larger still in the completed script.

The third great problem encountered by the television writer is the lay-out of the script. The difficulty is that, besides reading well as a piece of narrative, the script has to convey a good deal of technical information to the producer, the actors, the designer, the lighting-supervisor, the studio-manager and several other people. These two qualities are not necessarily complementary and a script may, for example, convey technical information quite adequately but read so badly as a narrative that it loses all chance of production. The best lay-out achieved so far, to my knowledge, was evolved by Robert Barr, the writer-producer of television documentaries until recently with the B.B.C. For simple reference I will call it the single-column lay-out. The main points are as follows:

(1) At the beginning of each scene the following information is given:

> The number of the scene.
> Whether it is live in the studio or filmed.
> Whether it is interior or exterior.
> Whether it is at night or by day.
> The set (if live); the location (if filmed).

(2) At the end of each scene there is a direction showing how it is to be linked to the next. If the scene ends a sequence the fact is stated. (A sequence is a group of scenes comparable to a chapter in a book or a movement in a symphony. It covers a complete stage in the development of the plot.)

(3) Stage and camera directions are set right across the page; dialogue is in-set.

40

Here is a brief example of the opening of a scene :

SCENE 16 STUDIO INT DAY PUBLIC BAR AT THE RAM HOTEL

Sam, the barman, comes in with a tray of newly washed glasses. He puts them on the bar and starts polishing them. Joe Hawkins comes in from the street.

SAM : Evening, Joe.
JOE : Evening, Sam.
SAM : Expected you here at six o'clock.
JOE : Couldn't help it. Working late.
SAM : Working? That's a fine one.

He draws Joe a drink.

And the end of the scene :

Sam picks up the message, looks at it a moment, then takes it through to the back parlour. As he goes through the door—

CUT TO—

SCENE 17 STUDIO INT DAY BACK PARLOUR AT THE RAM

If the scene had ended a sequence the direction would have read :

FADE — END OF SEQUENCE

Here is the script for a filmed scene :

SCENE 20 FILM EXT DAY HIGH STREET

The High Street is seen from Dr. Smith's house. It is morning and there is quite a lot of traffic. We pick up Dr. Smith's car as it turns off the road, comes into the short drive, and pulls up in front of the garage. Smith gets out and goes to the door. He is obviously agitated and fumbles with his door key. He unlocks the door. As he goes through—

CUT TO—

One of the advantages of this lay-out is that there is no doubt as to where a scene or sequence ends and where the next one begins. Nor can there be any doubt as to how the writer intends the scenes to be linked.

That deals, as far as it is possible to do so here, with the three main problems of the writer, but there are naturally others which vary with each programme. One difficulty, however, crops up so often that it should be given special mention; it is the difficulty of giving the appearance of continuous action or movement where actually there is a break.

Suppose that the action of a play or a dramatized documentary takes place in a block of offices. An employee, Jones, is having an interview with his boss, Robinson. The plot demands that Jones leaves Robinson and goes back immediately to his own office, where he is confronted with Brown. Sets for the connecting corridor together with the stairs have not been built and so the problem is to give the appearance of continuous movement and also allow Jones to walk from one set to the other. A possible solution is to continue the action in Robinson's office after Jones has left. Alternatively, Jones' secretary can ring through to speak to him on an urgent matter, to be told that he has just left. The telephone call will provide an opportunity to cut back to Jones' office and the action can continue there until his return.

There are several other solutions, but, whichever one is used, it is vital to write the short passages of dialogue bridging the time gap so that not a line is wasted. If they are not woven firmly into the plot, their original function will be only too obvious.

So far, in Britain, most original writing for television has been in the form of dramatized documentaries. As far as drama is concerned, we have done little to create a new television form and have lagged some way behind the Americans. In New York, writers like Paddy Chayefsky, Reginald Rose and Rod Serting, three leading American television playwrights, have been forging new patterns for the drama, suitable for the television medium. Chayefsky wrote *Marty*, the film version of which has had such a success both here and in America. Now that commercial television has arrived and new channels are opening, the opportunities for dramatic writing should increase enormously.

Television drama in Britain has clung too long to its theatrical origins, as if afraid to use its relative mobility, but slowly the apron strings are being untied and it now faces the task of establishing itself as a new, exciting and intelligent form in its own right. To do this, it must develop a new type of plot (just as the cinema did) and a new attitude towards its raw material. It is my contention that television drama should be taken from life in a more direct process than its theatrical counterpart; it should draw its subjects from the contemporary life of the nation and even snatch its plots from the daily newspapers.

Apart from drama, writers coming to television will find great scope in the various forms of the documentary: the dramatized documentary and the actuality and magazine documentaries. There is a large audience for these, as people today are fascinated by the lives and jobs of their fellow men and the complex chains of organizations and bodies, private or public, which affect them at every turn. It is no accident that a magazine like *The Strand*, which specialized in short stories, should have perished while dozens of periodicals devoted to factual articles continue to flourish.

Also it is being realized that there are more fascinating stories in the lives of apparently quite ordinary people than in most fiction, and television is an excellent medium for telling them. Documentaries such as *Can I Have a Lawyer?* by Jennifer Wayne, Robert Barr's *Medical Officer of Health* and Duncan Ross's *Course of Justice* series have demonstrated television's power to explain and make exciting subjects which, at first sight, might seem dull and obscure. John Grierson, the documentary producer, pointed out years ago that our democracy was becoming such an intricate piece of machinery that as individuals we were understanding it less and less. It seems to me that in the various forms of the documentary the writer of imagination can help to redress the balance.

I do not think anyone imagines that writing for television is an easy business; even for the writer who has succeeded in the theatre, the cinema, radio or elsewhere, there is a new technique to acquire and the difficult process of adapting a personal style to the needs of a complex medium. But it is my belief that the attempt is worth while, not only for the rewards of success, should they come, but also because it will introduce the writer to a new and exciting field of experience. Finally, it should be realized that television needs the writer even more than he needs television. Without him it can never grow to maturity, never deploy its latent power; and it can never be a wide, open and shining window on the world.

THE STORY DOCUMENTARY

CARYL DONCASTER

THE dramatized story documentary is one of the few art forms pioneered by television, stemming from the social films such as *Children on Trial, Out of True* and *Children of the City*. In the days soon after the war, that experimenter, Duncan Ross, in *The Course of Justice* series found a method of translating complex social problems into human terms in a way which caught and has continued to hold the imagination of the average television viewer.

From the point of view of entertainment, it is a fact that the most unrewarding social problems (such as, for example, the rehabilitation of the ex-prisoner, the subject of *Return to Living* which I wrote and produced), may, when presented in this dramatized form, rival the popularity of football or the Sunday night play. The facts of life so presented " get across " to a much wider section of the public than the straight talk. The talk informs. The dramatized story documentary interprets. One appeals to the intellect, the other to the emotions.

The story documentary, however, has very little in common with the straight drama, which depends for its effect on what the writer has to say, the strength of his plot with which he captivates our interest while he is saying it, and that " suspension of disbelief " which his audience must feel when watching, be it on the television set at home, at the theatre or in the cinema. The writer of the story documentary should never allow his own opinions on the subject he interprets to deflect him from impartiality. He must try to present each facet of the problem in true perspective.

As for plot, he is trying to present a cross-section of life; therefore, what plot he uses must only exist to give shape and

44

cohesion. He can never make use of *deus ex machina*, the happy ending, the numerous other theatrical devices which untie the knots. On the other hand, he is not trying to suspend the disbelief of his audience for, through his technique both as writer and producer, the viewer is presented with reality itself. Jean Anderson, the actress who portrayed the children's officer in *Children in Trust*, which showed how Local Government tackles the problem of the unwanted child, was approached in the street the day after the show by a woman who wanted her advice on one of her own children. James Hayter, after playing a Youth Club Leader in *Blunden's Club*, was asked to give a paper at a Youth Conference.

The successful writing of such documentaries depends in the first place on thorough research. Many a time trudging from town to town, trying to sift the heart of the matter from the differing viewpoints of all interested parties, I have envied the writer of plays, who is able to sit at home and conjure up character and situation from imagination. Research takes time and patience. For example, when writing *Return to Living*, I had first of all to " read up " the history and complicated theory relating to criminal conduct and prison reform and the complex rules and regulations governing H.M. Prisons. Only then did I tackle the experts, the Prison Commissioners, Governors and Officers. I visited prisons to meet prisoners on the point of re-entering the outside world. I talked to the " ex-lag " in his own haunts (needless to say the views expressed by ex-inmates of H.M. Prisons and those who govern them were in most instances contradictory). After about six weeks of journalistic delving I was faced with a mass of research notes, a blank piece of paper in the typewriter, a production deadline and the task of interpreting accurately the many-sided problem in dramatic form.

The method I have found that works most satisfactorily is to begin by wrestling with an outline giving the progression of action, number and type of characters, sets and film sequences required. This serves a number of purposes. It is useful at this early stage for practicalities like costing, design and the technical problems involved. It can be submitted to all interested parties so that minor inaccuracies of fact or emphasis can be corrected and any major points of disagreement thrashed out.

The dialogue script follows the outline. This, with further

minor amendments, will be used as the rehearsal script. To me this is the most enjoyable part of the writing. The most pressing worries of technique solved and unwieldy intractable material pushed into a shape, the characters then start coming to life. Sometimes more research is required over specialized dialogue. For instance, in *Return to Living* I enlisted the services of an old " lag " to turn what I wished to have said inside the prison into jail jargon.

Sometimes there is a temptation for the writer, as a newly fledged " expert," to include too many facts in the draft dialogue. True, the salient facts and theories leading to action should be included to inform the public, but they must be cleverly disguised so that the characters do not end by talking like textbooks. "When in doubt, leave out." The viewer can always get a textbook himself if sufficiently stimulated.

Another difficult discipline is to apportion the amount of weight given to each character and situation. Often the " odd man out " has a colourful story which it is tempting to built out of context. The central character of *Return to Living* was a Corrective Trainee whose crimes, sentences and future prospects of making good were average, and whose after-care showed best the work that is being done in this direction, though, as can be imagined, many of the stories related to me by members of the underworld were more colourful. Lesser characters were introduced to illustrate other facets of the after-care problem and the attitude of the public and officials to the ex-prisoner. It is these lesser characters, widening and enriching the canvas, that compensate in this type of script for lack of strong plot and often undramatic incident.

Final scripting can take anything up to two weeks before one enters the four-week production period. The writer-producer is always worried that his two functions may, owing to delay, overlap in time. It is the most difficult thing for me to write creatively (I am not including here script editing or limited rewriting) once I have switched to the production process. The fact is that a production of this kind demands a great deal of organizing ability to fit all requirements to the television machine.

Often, of course, the writer and producer are a two-person team, like the Ross-Atkins combination responsible for *The Course of Justice* series. There is a lot to be said for such team-

46

work. Writing and direction are such entirely different skills that they are not easily found in any one person, and a team of two can enrich the original conception in the cut-and-thrust of discussion. On the other hand, knowledge gained by the writer during research is a necessity during the production period for casting or designing sets (whose realism is often achieved by minute detail), and above all during the rehearsal period in order to help the actors achieve exact characterization.

The production of story documentaries is complicated by ordinary television standards and it makes heavy demands— a big studio, elaborate film sequences, large casts, multiple sets, the maximum number of camera, film and sound channels, complicated equipment moves. I am not suggesting by this that the production of a story documentary is more difficult than that of a drama. We do not have the " star " problem of casting, nor do our actors have to sustain performance to the same extent. Type casting, if great care is taken at the audition period, often means that an actor can walk into a small part with very little direction; nor are the camera-angles usually as complex as those demanded in the production of a play, where much ingenuity is often required to keep the pictorial element through complicated action. (The complications of cameras, etc., in a multi-set documentary occur chiefly in moves out of vision.) An intimate knowledge of both film and studio techniques is, however, required and it is better to cut one's teeth on other simpler types of production.

Once in a rehearsal room, routine does not differ radically from that facing the drama producer. During the first three days actors are positioned to cameras according to the shot breakdown, which has been prepared after consultation with the lighting-supervisor, the sound-engineer and the designer. For the next ten days lines are learnt and individual scenes are worked up. In order to cut costs on large casts, the whole company is not assembled after the first morning's " read through " until about four days before studio rehearsals, when an overall timing is taken and last-minute script and camera adjustments are made before the final camera script is duplicated.

During these four last days the experts are usually invited to the dingy rehearsal rooms to check performance and action for accuracy of detail. Where specialized action is required

47

they are called in sooner. For *The Call-up*, the War office lent a regimental sergeant-major to acquaint our juvenile actors with Army drill—an unrewarding job for the sergeant-major. In *Return to Living* I contented myself with a Home Office official and a representative " ex-lag "—whom we invited to visit us on different days!

The direction of actors for story documentaries differs a great deal from drama direction proper. An actor cannot " get by " by playing the character however skilled his technique. He has to " be " the person he is portraying. And to do this he has to forget most of the skills he has learned—his voice production technique, his movements, the projection of his own personality—everything by which he becomes a little larger than life must go. Nor is it enough to " underplay " the whole time, though this is the first requirement for television performance as a whole. It is a fact that the most successful documentary performances have often been given by young people with little or no previous training. These productions are popular with actors because they often graduate from them to drama proper.

Once lines and moves have been learned, I sometimes take the actor to meet the real people on whose activities the script is based. This usually alters their whole interpretation. In Jennifer Wayne's *Can I Have a Lawyer?* I took the whole cast to an East London Court. Thomas Heathcote, who most powerfully portrayed a Corrective Trainee in *Return to Living*, spent many hours talking to an ex-inmate of Dartmoor to get the feel of his character so that he might stop acting and become an ex-prisoner himself.

The cameras, too, can add or detract from the realism of the production. It is often a temptation to add to the drama of a situation by dramatic positioning of players to camera, by taking an unusual angle or using a dramatic cut. If this is done, the moment loses its validity, its human quality to which the viewer responds.

Writing and producing such story documentary programmes, while a member of a pioneer department of the B.B.C., was most stimulating and satisfying work. Our aim was simply to make human beings, their problems, ways of life and achievements more intelligible to other human beings in a way well suited to the tiny window of television.

DOCUMENTARY TV JOURNALISM

NORMAN SWALLOW

THE topical report is one form of the television documentary programme—its equivalent of *The March of Time*. To present its subject-matter in the most effective way possible it draws upon all the available resources of the medium—studios, film, outside broadcast points, back-projection, animated drawings, music, sound effects, tape-recordings, voices, professional experts and men-in-the-street, actors and non-actors. It can use commentators who are visible and those who are not; it demands patient research workers and script-writers who combine a high degree of professional skill with an ability to work fast and think faster. All these talents and resources, and others which may come along in the future, are blended as skilfully as possible to achieve a single purpose—the imaginative presentation of topical fact.

The producer, the man who does the blending, is as much a journalist as the writer of feature articles on a daily newspaper. Although he operates a machine which is infinitely more complex than a typewriter, his basic function remains the same. His qualifications, therefore, should be those of the good journalist everywhere; courage in his choice of subject-matter, honesty in his handling of it and imagination in his presentation of it; professional modesty; above all, integrity in his point of view.

To maintain these qualities in television is almost certainly more difficult than in any other form of journalism, so enormous is the impact of television and so great are the consequent pressures upon an extremely hard-worked individual. It is not easy to maintain a courageous choice of subject-matter—and, having chosen it, to handle it with ruthless honesty in the face

D

of an audience that is larger than the circulation of the most popular daily newspaper in the world. The power of television as propaganda is a phenomenon that is appreciated only too well by those who have a point of view to express and are naturally eager to ensure that their interests are neither ignored nor slighted before so large a public. To pursue the truth, and the truth alone, to give to each point of view and each " interest " as much space as it deserves (but no more) is often a tough task in this age of Public Relations Officers.

Imaginative presentation is a fine ideal, but it often seems very elusive to a man who is continually working against time. Content is always more important than method, and content takes up so much time and energy that method may tend to become automatic, routine and eventually second-rate. Professional modesty is never an easy quality for those who work in the glare of publicity; more publicity accompanies television at the present time than any other medium.

When B.B.C. Television first tried its hand at serious journalism its experiments took the form of the " personality " programme in a series called *Foreign Correspondent*, in which Chester Wilmot and Edward Ward presented personal reports, with film illustrations, of places they had visited on television assignments. Grace Wyndham Goldie, who produced these programmes, had clearly realized the value to the tiny home screen of three basic ingredients: the facts, the expert personality and the pictures of unfamiliar places that are in the news. Later she was to develop this technique until it became one of the main contributions to factual television, a style that allowed full scope for the talents of commentators like Christopher Mayhew and Aidan Crawley. It is a technique that will stay with us as long as television remains a " personality " medium . . . which will be for ever.

Yet the professional expert (the student of politics, the economist, the historian) is rarely a professional script-writer; he is untrained in the complex methods of writing for a medium where pictures count for more than words. When asked to prepare a television script he will usually write a verbal argument; at best he will write a long commentary and suggest the sort of pictures which might illustrate it. He will put words first and pictures second; he will call upon film sequences as a lecturer calls upon lantern slides. Consequently these sequences mean very little on their own without the accompanying argument. To a professional film-maker they have a superficial flavour about them; it could hardly be otherwise, for they are written by men who have probably had no experience in film editing, who have never seriously studied the emotional effects of certain combinations of image and sound, and so on. Whether the resulting programme stands or falls depends entirely on the force and integrity of the " expert " personality.

The film-maker is not necessarily right in his criticism, for the complete programme, with its dominating personality, is usually a professional job. Indeed, it would look a good deal less professional if the film sequences were really capable of making sense on their own. Any technical brilliance which they displayed would be in danger of contradicting the programme's main purpose—the projection of one man's personality, knowledge and ideas. The virtues of the producer of this kind of programme are the virtues of self-denial. His sole concern is to use television as a technical method of expressing a personality, and that personality must never be his own.

Special Enquiry: a Report for Television, which the B.B.C. began in 1952, was an attempt to break away from the " personality " approach, to find a new way of handling similar subject-matter. The professional expert was replaced by the enquiring reporter, a man whose initial knowledge is no greater than that of the viewer on whose behalf he conducts the enquiry. He never dominates the programme; for most of its length he is only a voice speaking words that are slightly more personal than those of a film commentator. He adopts no personal thesis and postulates no argument. He moves from place to place, using his film camera as a reporter might use his notebook and pencil. He asks the questions that a sensible layman would ask. He never presumes to pass judgment on the answers.

By using a man who claimed no particular knowledge of the subject-matter, there was no obligation to let him dominate the proceedings. His function was largely structural; he was the fixed point of the enquiry, the man through whose eyes and ears the viewer absorbed the story. Not that he was a mere " stooge "; most of the reporters in the series have been journalists of distinction in other fields—Edward Ward, René Cutforth, Colin Wills, Jean Metcalfe—and they have always determined the general line of approach, the people to be questioned, the locations to be visited, and so on. They have used their professional skill as interviewers, and their individual literary styles have given a personal touch to the final commentary.

But—and this is the important point—in this form of documentary journalism the script is not the work of the reporter alone. He is merely a member of a script-writing team which includes a professional television writer in addition to the programme's producer and director. The aims of this team are to write a report with the maximum of pictures and the minimum of words; to work out the most effective combination of image and sound to produce the correct balance of forceful argument and emotional power (it is a characteristic of the personality programme, that its emotional content is so small: the appeal is usually to the head and only rarely to the heart); and to achieve these ends by the wisest possible use of the available resources. This is a complicated business and one which is clearly beyond the powers of the journalist whose training has so far been in Fleet Street or Broadcasting House. The newspaper reporter can collect his material with a pencil and notebook, the radio reporter can achieve his results with a portable tape-recorder; but the television reporter is one man in a large team.

Television journalism, like film journalism, means closely knit teamwork; and the good team will work well together, each member contributing his own specialized skill to an agreed result. The producer's function is to ensure that this result has the appearance of a well-made, smooth-running vehicle, rather than a tattered cart that is pulled by several ill-mannered horses, each facing a different direction (a danger, of course, which is avoided by the programme that is dominated by a single personality). If any individual style can be traced in the documentary type of journalism it will be that of the producer, the leader of the team.

The fundamental decisions on subject-matter, general method and point of view rest largely with the producer. At the back of his mind, as he makes these decisions, will be his awareness of television's impact as a social force. Television is the most potent means of social propaganda so far invented; in 1954 some six million people in Britain watched each programme by Christopher Mayhew and each edition of *Special Enquiry*. If this gives tremendous power to the documentary producer, it should also serve to remind him of his responsibilities; for irresponsibility in television is unpardonable. This is the atmosphere in which the producer-journalist works and it should condition his attitude towards his task.

Because the machine which he drives is powerful, he ought not to waste it on trivialities. He should choose his subjects with his eyes firmly fixed on their social value; a democracy should be well and truthfully informed, and he is in charge of its most powerful single source of information. At the same time he must not be frightened by his responsibilities—he must not lose courage. The most important subjects, precisely because they are so important, are always those which tread on the toes of certain influential sections of the community. Treading on toes requires courage, but tread on them he must. The producer who treads on all of them without prejudice in his single-minded pursuit of the truth has nothing to fear. If, on the other hand, he allows himself to be pushed aside into an evasion of delicate issues then his final production will be dishonest and he deserves to lose his job.

He needs courage, certainly. He also needs a deep sense of responsibility. The half-truth, the surrender to a personal bias (and we all have them), these are as dangerous as cowardice, are indeed another form of cowardice. If his programme presents the truth as he sees it, then he has done all he can. If he fails in this one ambition, then he fails utterly.

All this presupposes one essential condition : that he is completely trusted by the organization which employs him. He works too quickly to be able to submit every point to higher authority. Every day will bring its share of delicate decisions; to make them with confidence he must feel that they will be defended (in public, if need be) by those who employ him. Ed Murrow's programme on Senator McCarthy presupposed the support of the Columbia Broadcasting System. The *Special Enquiry* into the colour bar in Britain presupposed the complete support of the B.B.C. Mutual confidence between the broadcasting organization and the individual producer is essential. Without it there can be no honest television reporting at all. (If I may state a personal opinion, it is no coincidence that in the two networks with the finest world reputation for their handling of current events this mutual confidence exists to a high degree.)

Here is a list of some of the subjects which have so far been tackled by *Special Enquiry* in an attempt to combine an outspoken pursuit of the truth with a sincere sense of social responsibility: housing, unemployment, smoke pollution, illiteracy, old age, Britain's roads, Cyprus and Enosis, the colour bar, German rearmament, health, National Service, teen-agers. They all have certain factors in common: they are social problems; they are issues on which the British record, as a democratic community, is not as perfect as it might be; they are subjects which have inflamed all manner of partisan passions, so that the truth is hard to find, but equally well worth the finding; they are all subjects which lend themselves to pictorial treatment.

They are also subjects which demand location treatment. Consequently the bulk of each programme has been filmed in places where people can be shown in the context of their social problems and can be called upon to discuss them: the slum dwellers of Glasgow, the smog-bound citizens of Manchester in December, Jamaican immigrants in a puzzled Birmingham. These are the places where drama lies, a drama as powerful as anything that can be created by a writer in his study, a drama that gains in intensity by the fact of being true. Looking back over the series in the last four years I find, not surprisingly, that the most vivid memories are of the simple, unscripted statements by ordinary people: the mother in the Glasgow slum who stood in the rain-soaked backyard and said her children were so used to the rats that they were learning to play with them; the white wife of a West African immigrant who said she had the best husband in the world; the Devonshire villagers who met in the local school-room and demanded to know why their school was being closed; always the simple, human drama played by the real people in the real environment.

The world is a much smaller place than it used to be; it is no longer possible for us to think of our own national problems in isolation. Events in Bangkok are of more than academic interest to the citizens of Burnley. Whether our motives are altruistic or purely selfish we would be wise to keep an eye on the other end of the world. This is as true of social matters as it is of politics.

With this in mind, the B.B.C. started in April, 1954, another series of journalistic documentaries called *The World is Ours*. Their aim is to report on the battle being fought by the specialized agencies of the United Nations—WHO, FAO, ILO, Unesco and others—against poverty, ignorance, hunger and disease. They also have the equally important purpose of showing that in a divided world it is still possible for men of different nationalities, religions and political opinions to work together constructively and at peace.

The World is Ours, unlike *Special Enquiry*, is part of an already well-established tradition. It springs directly from those post-war documentary films which had the same broad purpose, *The World is Rich* and *World Without End*; nor is it a coincidence that the television series was initiated by Paul Rotha, then Head of Documentaries for the B.B.C. Television Service. Although it began as a part-studio, part-film series, it has been made entirely on celluloid since its third issue. Its production, which will run to twelve programmes of forty-five minutes each, is made with the collaboration of the U.N. Films Division in New York.

Its strength lies in the tradition from which it springs and to which it owes a well-proved technique and a sound crusading zeal. Its weaknesses are the consequence of transferring that tradition to television; in its efforts to translate to the small home screen what was essentially a technique for the cinema it has perhaps failed to evolve a form that is entirely satisfactory for its new medium. Moreover, it can hardly avoid comparison with films that were made at a quarter of the speed and with twenty times the money. It cannot fail to suffer from such a comparison, but so far its basic inspiration has seen it through. It is an important series, not only as an example of social propaganda at its most constructive, but also because, as an international series, it provides opportunities for film and television technicians of many countries to work together on subject-matter which affects them all.

This essay has tried to avoid technicalities, partly because the technical problems in all forms of television tend to be similar, but also because, in documentary journalism, the virtues of the journalist are almost certainly more important than those of the television technician. It has been proved that the television audience for good journalism is large and enthusiastic. Here is a type of programme for which there will always be a market and whose social value is unquestioned.

OUTSIDE TELEVISION BROADCASTS

PETER DIMMOCK

IN the televising of actual events as they take place in reality, television is being used in its most basic form. The unexpected happening in sport, the unrehearsable incident at a public occasion, the deployment of cameras at points of the greatest strategic visual importance—these are the stuff with which the outside broadcast television producer works and which make his job perhaps the most exciting in television.

The producer operates from a mobile control-room, parked sometimes hundreds of yards from the location where the event is to take place. He cannot enjoy that event; all he sees are the pictures being picked up by the various television cameras and shown on the monitor screens spread out in front of his control desk. This desk has a shaded light for the producer's script, a microphone through which he can direct and co-ordinate his cameras and commentators, and a row of buttons which he presses to change from camera to camera as the programme evolves. This control-room has to be as small as possible in order to make parking less of a problem. In it, as well as the complicated electronic equipment and monitor screens, work the technicians under a crew chief who is responsible to the producer for all the technical arrangements and the quality of the pictures being transmitted.

Perhaps more than any other quality, a television outside broadcast man must have a solid news sense to combine with any artistic sense that he may use in his productions. His main job is to report events and facets of real life in pictures and sound. He must try not to miss any of the essential action and to achieve so far as possible a sense of participation in the event for those who are viewing. Where he really comes into his own in the United Kingdom is at big public and State occasions. The B.B.C. Television Service has covered all the big State occasions in Britain since the war.

Perhaps the simplest way of describing the work of an outside broadcast television producer is to tell the story in some detail of the most famous B.B.C. telecast to date, the Coronation of Queen Elizabeth on June 2nd, 1953, seen by over 20 million people in Great Britain and by many millions in Europe, as well as by countless millions more after the event by tele-recorded film.

A few months before the Coronation, I was sent by the then Head of O.B's. to the United States, this time to watch American television's coverage of President Eisenhower's Inauguration and Parade in Washington. I returned to London in February, 1953, and at once got down to the job of selecting our camera positions on the Coronation route and in Westminster Abbey for what was clearly to be one of television's greatest events. We could not have received more co-operation from the officials of the Ministry of Works, especially the architects who had to convert our technical requirements for camera stands and rostrums into something that would harmonize with the general decorative scheme along the route.

The three most difficult outdoor positions were the Victoria Memorial, Grosvenor Gate at Hyde Park and outside the Abbey Approach. The demands on space at the Victoria Memorial facing Buckingham Palace were from sound broadcasters (home and overseas), newsreel and colour film cameramen, still-photographers, Army signallers, several hundred schoolchildren and ourselves. From television's point of view it was a particularly strategic position because we were determined to have a camera set-up from which we could obtain a long-held close-up of the Queen immediately she left the Palace on the most eventful day of her life. As it transpired, we captured her smile in close-up as the golden coach started its journey to the Abbey. This shot was taken by a cameraman in gumboots on a rostrum built (by special permission) in the fountain on the edge of the Victoria Memorial itself. He was supported by another camera inside the forecourt of the Palace, and a third one on the roof looking directly down the Mall.

The next problem was to cover the procession through Hyde Park. In consultations with the Army we were advised that, when the Queen left Westminster Abbey after the ceremony, the head of the procession would be somewhere between Stanhope Gate and Grosvenor Gate. Even a few weeks before Coronation Day it was impossible to determine its exact position and so we were faced with the dilemma of either putting our cameras at Marble Arch—because I had observed in Washington that processions should be covered as nearly as possible head-on and from slightly above—or at the side of East Carriage Drive in Hyde Park. But the Marble Arch site was out. The procession, because of its great size, could not pass through the centre arch without splitting into three groups. We therefore settled for a position north of Grosvenor Gate.

The problem outside Westminster Abbey itself was to find somewhere high from which to see both the roadway outside the Abbey and at the same time catch a glimpse of Parliament Square and Big Ben. An obvious vantage point was the top of Abbey House, but it did not look from the pavement, eighty-five feel below, that there was a flat roof to the building. We scrambled out through a tiny skylight on to a series of precarious and steep roofs. Chimneys poked up to obstruct the view and it was not very promising. We decided, however, that there was one possible camera position, only to find that the Newsreel Association of the film industry had beaten us to it. We then called in our tubular-scaffolding experts. They agreed that a temporary platform could be fastened just below roof level. This was the point from which the high pictures outside Westminster Abbey were taken.

With all our outside camera positions finally decided, the various mobile units and their crews were allocated to their respective sites, together with an outside broadcast producer for each one. It was the producer's job to fix technical details with our engineering planners, who, in conjunction with the Post Office, the London Electricity Board and the Ministry of Works, were arranging for the equipment installation, sound lines and vision circuits. Alternative routes had to be planned so as to reduce the chances of a serious breakdown to the minimum. At this stage, the then Head of Outside Broadcasts decided that I should produce the television broadcast of the ceremony from inside the Abbey itself.

The first thing to do, as always, was to find suitable camera positions. This is never easy. Westminster Abbey was not

58

built with a view to the possible requirements of television cameras, newsreels, colour films, still-photographers, broadcasters and the like. Space is at an absolute premium and, as the " new boy," television merely adds another problem for the hard-pressed architects who had designed the film camera-booths for the 1937 Coronation. Where only one camera had operated then, the space in 1953 was divided into two and at once nicknamed the " dog kennels " by the cameramen who were to sit in them from the early hours until after the Queen had left the Abbey in the afternoon. We carried out exhaustive tests beforehand and our technicians designed and built, back at our Wembley base, special camera mountings and full-scale positions, so as to ensure the best possible operational coverage by each camera through its small peephole.

Our major problem was to decide the best way of covering a complex ceremony lasting nearly two hours, which required watching from four opposite ends and sides of the Abbey. For example, the position offered to us high in the Triforium afforded an excellent bird's-eye view of St. Edward's Chair, the Throne and the Theatre west of the Altar. You could not, however, from this position see either the Altar itself or the area immediately in front of it. The Earl Marshal authorized another position for us in the corner of the South-west Transept, but even from here it was not possible to see the whole of the Altar or the Chair of Estate. The position above the tombs in the sanctuary was already promised to the colour film camera-men, so—where was television to go?

The Choir Screen would be crammed to capacity with the finest orchestra in Great Britain. The Earl Marshal and Sir William McKie, Director of Music for the Coronation, were prepared to agree to our request for a camera beside the Organ Console provided that it was fixed and had no operator with it. My primary aim in using the cameras was to achieve audience participation rather than merely to watch the ceremony as if it were a pageant. It was therefore important to achieve some sort of operation for the Choir Screen camera, even if only to have someone beside it to change the lenses. Nothing destroys the sense of participation more than a wide-angle picture containing a lot of small detail in addition to the main action.

Sir William McKie thought it might be possible for an operator to sit beneath the fixed camera to turn the lens turret. This

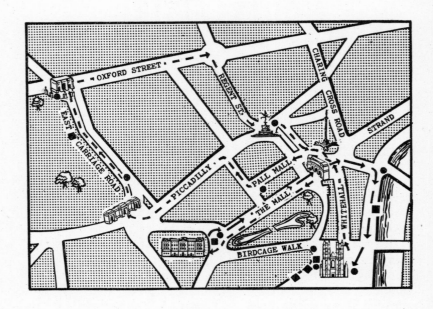

THE CORONATION OF QUEEN ELIZABETH II, JUNE 2nd, 1953

Above. Map showing the route taken by the procession from Buckingham Palace to Westminster for the Ceremony and the return afterwards to the Palace.

The positions of the B.B.C. television live Outside Broadcast cameras are shown thus ■

B.B.C. sound radio commentators positions shown thus ●

Page 61. Plan of the Abbey interior showing positions of the five cameras used to cover the ceremony.

Cameras 1 and 2 are in the Triforium to cover the Theatre west of King Edward's Chair. Camera 3 is concealed in the Transept. Camera 4 is fitted beside the Organ on the Choir Screen. Camera 5 is hidden above the West Door to cover the processions west of the Choir Screen.

The Producer's control-room (not shown on plan) is located outside the building on the south-east side of the Triforium.

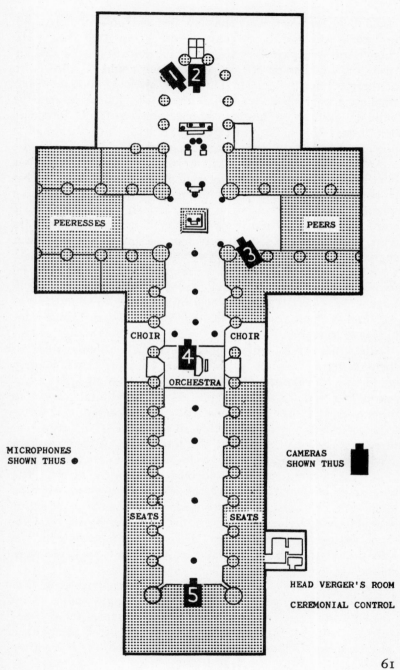

PEERESSES

PEERS

CHOIR

CHOIR

ORCHESTRA

SEATS

SEATS

MICROPHONES
SHOWN THUS ●

CAMERAS
SHOWN THUS

HEAD VERGER'S ROOM

CEREMONIAL CONTROL

could not, however, be definitely decided until the first full orchestra rehearsal, a few days before Coronation Day. The chances of giving viewers a sense of participation depended entirely on whether or not our cameraman could be allowed to be there. " Bud " Flanagan, five feet in his socks and one of our smallest cameramen, was chosen for the job. He met Sir William and the orchestra's manager on the Choir Screen to demonstrate his ability to screw himself up into the smallest possible space on the floor. It was agreed.

At last the rehearsal day arrived. With Flanagan we climbed the Choir Screen stairs to find that there did not appear to be room even for all the music stands. In the precise spot where we had hoped Flanagan would crouch, there was a music stand and the point of a 'cello! Sir William and the orchestra were polite but the situation seemed an impasse until it was suggested that by raising the camera slightly it might be possible for Eugene Pini, the 'cellist, to pass his bow under it, and for the point of the 'cello to be placed between Flanagan's feet. Eugene Pini was prepared to help in any way he could, and so we built a small perch on the side of the Organ Console for Flanagan to sit on.

Altogether we had five cameras inside the Abbey, three of them covering various parts of the Theatre. Each camera could take four different lenses varying between angles of about one degree and forty-five degrees in the horizontal plane. In other words, a one degree lens will give a close-up, and forty-five degree lens a wide-angle view of the scene. Unfortunately there is one big problem for the television outside broadcast producer: the wide- and narrow-angle lenses at the extremities of the range cannot be simultaneously used in the turret. The wide-angle lens sees the end of the longer narrow-angle lens in its picture. Usually a compromise has to be made, although it is sometimes possible for the operator to change lenses between shots during the programme. This was not possible in the Abbey, but, though the close-up lenses were barred, we were able to achieve a fair range of lens angles.

The camera over the West Door was fitted with a British-made zoom lens by means of which the angle could be increased or decreased at the ratio of five-to-one from the original starting angle. It was this camera which appeared to hold the Queen almost stationary as she proceeded down the Nave after the ceremony. In fact, the Queen covered a distance of about twenty-five yards while the electrical operation of the zoom lens kept her the same size on the screen. Eventually Ken Mackay, the operator of this camera, could not zoom out any further so he panned gently down and then allowed the Queen to pass out of sight at the bottom of the screen. He did not pan down too steeply as experience has shown that this merely causes the viewer to lose perspective on the rest of the procession at the back.

Pre-transmission briefings between the producer and the outside broadcast cameramen, engineers and commentator are vital before any transmission because the success of a programme depends on teamwork. It also calls for a kind of telepathy between producer, commentator and cameramen so that pictures and words can flow smoothly together.

I had already had the pleasure of producing several outside broadcasts with Richard Dimbleby as commentator and we had achieved an understanding that seemed to give each of us a sixth sense of anticipation. I had only to speak one quick sentence, or even a single word, for him to grasp fully my meaning and provide the necessary words to cover the picture. For example, one of the most important tasks of an outside broadcast producer is to ask his commentator to lead him from picture to picture, particularly when you are changing to a camera in another position. The commentator is then the vital link for the viewer at his set.

During the Abbey service, Dimbleby frequently " dotted the i " and, when we obtained our shot of the Duke of Cornwall watching his mother being crowned, I was able to give Dimbleby a quick verbal tap on the shoulder over my " talk-back " microphone. Having seen the shot on pre-view, I said, " Have a picture of Charles, will cut as soon as you mention him." I had always hoped to be able to televise Prince Charles at the precise time of his mother's crowning. This seemed to me to be one of the most significant moments of our history : our future King watching this ancient ceremony which he himself may one day enact.

An experienced outside broadcast commentator must also be master of the unexpected situation. In our preview of the Abbey scene, we had arranged to spend a few moments identifying some of the principal foreign personalities in the Choir

Stalls before the arrival of the royal processions. Just as we reached the Choir Stalls, Camera 2 warned me that Princess Margaret was about to come through the Choir Screen. I warned Dimbleby and he was able to cover with words the movement of the camera as it swung to the right to pick up the Princess's entry. His words: "Now everyone stands, as well they might, because Princess Margaret now moves into the Theatre." Just a few simple words of explanation, but enough to reassure viewers that the camera was moving away from the Choir Stalls for a purpose.

Another important aspect of an outside broadcast producer's job is sound coverage. He must discuss with the mobile unit's senior technician in charge of the crew and the sound-mixer the best possible microphone coverage that will help sound to match picture. Much of this is done weeks beforehand when the producer visits the site with a planning-engineer whose job it is to make a record of all the producer's technical requirements and to arrange the necessary power and Post Office circuits for the television broadcast. Inevitably, however, much of the detail has to be decided on the site with the sound-engineer.

In the case of the Coronation Service we were taking the B.B.C. radio sound coverage before, of course, it was mixed with its separate commentary. This is called a "clean feed." Where both sound radio and television are covering an event together, this method avoids unnecessary duplication of microphones.

In the Abbey, in addition to the B.B.C. sound radio feed, we had two microphones for our own exclusive use. One was a general effects microphone high in the roof; the other was to cover the Homage. While this part of the ceremony takes place, the orchestra and choir fill the Abbey with fortissimo music. Because of this tremendous sound, radio decided not to record the dialogue of the Homage at the 1937 Coronation, but instead to let their commentator describe the words being spoken. I was not keen to adopt this method for television because it seemed illogical that we should show the Homage without hearing the words being spoken, however faintly, behind the singing and music. It was agreed that midget microphones of the latest type should be concealed on the sides of the throne. None of us knew until the actual day whether they would in fact pick up the vital words.

64

To the day itself. We reported by 6.30 a.m. at our thirty-foot square control-room, specially built adjoining the King Henry VII Chapel outside the Abbey. After checking technical details with the three senior engineers, I climbed the spiral turret stone staircase high into the Triforium. There I joined Richard Dimbleby in his soundproof commentary box to decide precisely how we would cover the opening scene. Although we had a pre-determined plan, it was not until the Abbey was filled that we could really decide the exact order in which we would switch from camera to camera, or those things which we would show in close view as Dimbleby explained how the service would unfold later that morning.

It was vital to get as much as possible of this explanation over to the viewer in the preliminary visit because there would not be time to explain it during the actual Service. It was also imperative to keep the amount of commentary during the ceremony to an absolute minimum. Above all, it had to be timed perfectly so as not to clash with the spoken words of the Service itself.

As usual, there were the last-minute rumours common to all great occasions. You think that every eventuality has been foreseen, but suddenly you are told that the National Anthem is to be played for the Queen Mother's procession. This seemed unlikely, but it had to be checked. The only man who could discover the exact facts was " Bud " Flanagan at our Choir Screen camera in the middle of the orchestra. He could not, however, speak back to us in the control-room, but he did have on a pair of head-phones in order to receive the producer's instructions in one ear and the programme sound in the other. (This is very important as the cameraman must, in addition to hearing the producer, be able to hear the commentator so that if necessary he can pan his camera in perfect time with the commentary. This leaves the producer free to concentrate on preparing another camera ready for the next sequence.) I picked up Dimbleby's microphone and the sound-mixer faded it up so that Flanagan could hear me. I asked him to find out about the Anthem and the Queen Mother. It was essential that he should remain unobtrusive, so he pulled his ear for " yes " and smoothed his hair for " no." Needless to say, the rumour was false.

Returning to the control-room, we briefly ran through the

E

opening sequence with cameras and fed it through to the central television switching centre at Broadcasting House so that they could see the picture quality and check the sound circuit. After this, we rested the cameramen and technicians while for the last time we went through our script and made sure that we knew exactly where the difficult lens-change sequences came. This was important because the cameramen had to be particularly quick at these points in order to avoid any possible breaking of the mood or sense of participation which we hoped to obtain during the whole broadcast. This done, it left the engineers free to have their final technical line-up tests. Then we all waited for the historic outside broadcast to begin.

At 10.15 everyone was alert. Those of us in the control-room fixed our eyes on the screen, which showed Sylvia Peters making the opening announcement. Then the picture changed to scenes outside Buckingham Palace. Phase One of Television Operation Coronation Day had begun. The weather was far from kind, but nothing could spoil this day. Soon the Queen was on her way down the Mall. Viewers were taken ahead of the Procession to watch the arrival of Princess Margaret and the Queen Mother outside Westminster Abbey.

Tension mounted in our control-room. The cameramen, squeezed in their little boxes, prepared for the moment when live television pictures of the scene inside Westminster Abbey on Coronation Day would be transmitted throughout Great Britain and to many parts of Europe. Staffs in film laboratories were alert to receive negative for immediate processing. Jet aircraft and B.O.A.C. Stratocruisers were standing by waiting to rush film telerecordings, taken directly off the television tube, to Canada and the U.S.A.

For those of us who were members of the B.B.C. team—and I cannot over-stress that it was wholly a team effort—responsible for the Abbey television broadcast, the most anxious moment of all came when Michael Henderson, the commentator at the Colonial Office, gave the cue, " And so let us join Richard Dimbleby with our cameras inside Westminster Abbey." Instantly our minds concentrated on the production as history began to unfold on the five monitor screens before us. When we had finished this preliminary transmission, and watched Princess Margaret and the Queen Mother's Processions move to the Royal Box, we handed back to one of the mobile units outside

66

the Abbey—this time to the Embankment, where a great welcome was being given to the Queen by thousands of London schoolchildren.

Now we waited for the supreme moment. Returning to the Abbey, viewers would see the start of the Grand Procession and the beginning of the most glorious ceremony in Britain's history. The ban on big close-ups was in accord with the B.B.C.'s normal practice at religious services.

I had now to keep one eye on the transmission monitor which showed the actual picture being sent into viewers' homes, and the other on the four pictures being pre-viewed on the other cameras' control channels. Unlike studio technique, where usually the actors play to the various cameras in accordance with the producer's directions at rehearsal, the outside broadcast producer often finds his camera positions limited to certain defined areas. He must therefore always be prepared to keep his shooting-script flexible so that, if an alternative camera can provide a better view, he must at once seize the opportunity to put it on transmission. This is, of course, provided that it does not threaten to spoil the rhythm of the whole television broadcast. The outside broadcast producer must be careful about this opportunism because it would obviously be foolish to miss a planned shot later on.

Throughout the service, the then Head of Religious Broadcasting's helpful prompting was invaluable. I could concentrate on the production while he followed the service. He prompted me about events to come so that there was little risk of my getting lost by concentrating on obtaining a particular good shot at any given moment.

Although an outside broadcast cameraman's viewfinder contains a pilot cue-light to warn him when his camera is being used by the producer for transmission, it is essential for the producer to keep him fully informed about the progress of the programme. This is the kind of monologue that I could have been heard making over the " talk-back " circuit during the Abbey transmission: " Coming to you Cam. 3 on your 8-inch, centre the Regalia, please; Cams. 3 and 4, am matching you both; stand by, Richard: am going closer on the Regalia centring the Crown. Right; MIX on you Cam. 3, change to your 4-inch Cam. 4 and give me a reserve wide angle." (This in case Cam. 3 should develop a fault, or prove to be a little too close to include

67

all the action of the particular sequence.) "Coming to you next Cam. 6 as the procession turns past the Throne—8-inch, please; stay wide Cam. 5, shall only use you if I'm in trouble on 3 or 4. Warn me when the Queen is reaching the Choir Screen Cam. 2." (This to the camera operator over the West Door who could see up the Nave towards the Choir Screen.) "Shall take the procession fairly wide on you Cam. 3 for the Queen's entrance and then a little closer on you Cam. 4 as the Vivats begin. Stand by Cam. 6, the Regalia is turning towards you—MIX—hold it still and let them go through Cam. 6. Coming to you Cam. 3 . . ." and so on.

How does the commentator know whether the producer's directions refer to him or the cameramen? This is done by a spring-loaded key on the producer's desk which is pressed only when he wants the commentator to hear him. Sometimes it saves time to feed an experienced commentator with producer's talk-back all the time, but as a general rule it is much better to cause the commentator as little interruption as possible. He should only be told essentials. During the Abbey Service my instructions to Richard Dimbleby were kept to an absolute minimum in order not to distract his train of thought and flow of delivery.

The whole outside television broadcast of the Coronation remains an unforgettable memory for those of us associated with it. The cameramen did a splendid and sensitive job in most difficult circumstances. Every credit is due, in common with all the other television mobile unit locations on that day, to the dozens of electronic engineers, both B.B.C. and Post Office, whose backroom work ensured that the pictures picked up by the cameras were reproduced faithfully and instantaneously in homes as far apart as Belfast and Berlin.

BALLET, OPERA AND MUSIC

PHILIP BATE

IN any television organization the Music Department must be one of the most interesting if only because of the variety of material and diversity of opinion which come within its bounds. Certainly this is so in B.B.C. Television, where, after nine years of public service (disregarding for the moment the very important experiments of 1936-39), members of the Music Department disagree with each other on many matters as handsomely as ever they did. This is healthy.

Within the larger framework of B.B.C. Television as a whole, the Music Department has a dual function. It is both a service and a creative body. In the first capacity it is the source of supply on which all the other departments indent for their practical needs in music from the engagement of a symphony orchestra to the purchase of a penny whistle. At the same time it provides a point of reference where expert musical advice may always be had.

To these ends, the Department maintains large music and gramophone record libraries, which also draw on the main B.B.C. libraries as well as the hiring departments of the various music publishers. It provides also for the commissioning of special music when required, for arranging and copying and for the hire of musical instruments. All this, in itself, is sufficient to occupy a considerable staff, and some television organizations prefer to keep their service and programme production sections entirely separate. In Great Britain, however, musical offerings of a serious type are allotted a greater proportion of programme time by the B.B.C. than in most other countries, and in these circumstances the dual department seems to have practical advantages.

On the creative side the work of a television music unit is much less easy to define, but perhaps it may help if we begin by thinking for a moment about music itself. Music is the most persuasive of all emotional stimulants. Music, besides being an end in itself, complete and perfect, has through the ages been the servant of public entertainment and the support of religious ceremony. There are a hundred ways in which music can serve and enhance the visual experience. It is, therefore, only natural that music should maintain its long-accepted functions in the new medium of television.

The matter becomes even clearer if we recall that basically television is—at least, in my opinion—no more than an extension of the now familiar every-day radio. Sight has been added to sound over the air as some thirty years ago sound was added to sight in the moving-picture theatre. In spite of the excitement and false evaluation that this novelty engendered for a time in a public accustomed only to sound radio, there is essentially no more to it than this. We now have a medium of distant communication that employs the senses of sight and hearing in their normal relation to each other.

Accepting what has been set out in the previous paragraphs, it is obvious that among the many forms of entertainment civilized man has developed there are two which television by its very nature cannot ignore—ballet and opera. Both are composite arts. In both music is an essential ingredient, and it is in these two fields that much of the early and most important television experiment was made.

At first sight ballet would appear to be almost the ideal ready-made camera material; in fact, it is frequently the most difficult of subjects to realize with integrity on the screen; very occasionally it is the most rewarding. In the earliest days, in the minute studios which were all that were available for experiment at the B.B.C., ballet could only be represented by solo dances or perhaps an occasional *pas de deux*. These were taken from the classics or specially created, and were often performed by distinguished dancers, for even then some artistes realized how important the new medium would one day become to them.

With the opening by the B.B.C. in 1936 of rather more adequate television studios it became possible to call on existing ballet companies, such as the Vic-Wells, Ballet Rambert or the

70

De Basil Ballet Russe, and to present more or less complete items. At this stage a certain amount of special creation was also going on, but quite naturally repertory material became for a time the main source of supply.

The situation was further influenced by the fact that at that time the television audience, though small by present-day standards, was well accustomed to the theatre and took ballet as part of its normal theatrical fare. Special outside broadcast equipment which could be taken into commercial theatres was comparatively undeveloped, so the television producer's job was to present ballet from the studio in a manner acceptable to a largely theatre-conditioned audience. Not an easy problem, but a clearly defined one.

When post-war television began in Britain in 1946, conditions had changed greatly. An entirely new audience had grown up with different ideas and different standards. Our former assessment no longer held good. Outside broadcast equipment slowly became available, and almost at once certain pre-conceived ideas were demolished. It became evident that a camera placed in the best stall in the theatre gives on the home screen a very pale shadow of the experience that the live individual sitting in the same seat will build up for himself. Several cameras with different characteristics of focal length, angle of coverage, etc., are required to achieve a bare approximation, and even then the will of the producer alone dictates which camera is active at any given moment.

This is a long way from the instantaneous and unconscious adjustment of a pair of living eyes and the receptive brain behind them. We had begun, in fact, to realize the importance of individual psychology and physiology in the members of an audience.

To get the best results on the home screen, major adjustments to stage groups, directions of movements, etc., may be called for, and often these are quite incompatible with the requirements of a large proscenium production. It follows then that at present the studio remains the best place even for televised "theatre" ballet, for there the necessary adjustments can be made freely. Happily they are no longer dictated by mere lack of space.

It will be noted that the previous sentences imply the existence of another type of screened ballet, and this has grown up

71

rapidly in post-war years. It is best distinguished by the term "television" ballet, and here we have perhaps the ultimate future of dancing for the home screen. Here none of the shibboleths of an older art need apply. The only canons to be observed are those of good taste.

The basic material is, of course, the dancer, but beyond his or her technical training the producer and choreographer need owe nothing to the traditional dance theatre. Every possible technical device of lighting, staging, mobile or multiple viewpoints, etc., is permissible provided that it contributes to the forceful telling of the story, and trick camera-work (which is only legitimate in very special cases in theatre ballet) can be fully exploited. Indeed, in this type of work the camera itself may well become the star of the production. There is only one danger—it is all too easy to become so drunk with one's technical cleverness as to obscure one's own object. In this, as in all arts, we must, therefore, rely on good taste and self-discipline.

To round off this section, let us see how a producer sets about televising a ballet. So many and diverse are the factors that a full description is impossible: but in partial answer I quote a paragraph from an article I wrote for *Ballet Annual* some years ago, but which I believe still to hold good.

"First and most important, he (the producer) must analyse closely. Is the chosen ballet one in which the story is told primarily by means of mass movements, or does it depend upon the interaction of one or two clearly defined characters? Is the emotional content inherent in the overall pattern? If the latter, it is likely that the producer will feel obliged to choose shots of such a length that the pattern as a whole is not in any way mutilated; and here is a case where present-day limitations may get in his way, because the ability of the camera at the moment to resolve fine detail does fall off rather sharply at a certain critical distance from its subject.

"On the other hand, where subsidiary dancers may perhaps be used chiefly as a living background or as commentators upon the relationship of the principal characters, he may be wise to concentrate upon the principals to the exclusion of almost everything else.

"Having made this decision to his own satisfaction, the producer must next consider carefully the type of background which will be most helpful, and this it must be admitted may not necessarily be the one which was most effective in the theatre. I would go so far as to say that there are some ballets at the present time being presented in the theatre—because the theatre is the traditional home of ballet—which in fact gain greatly in impact from the selectivity which the camera gives. In such cases, where there are comparatively few characters, all well defined, the producer will try to use a series of shots and angles which will bring out the drama to the fullest extent.

"Happily there are at the present time a number of choreographers of imagination who appreciate what the camera can do for them, and who are prepared to compose with this medium always in mind. For them I believe television holds a big future. In time television choreographers must take over some of the questions that at present fall to the lot of the producer. The choreographer will decide where large patterns rather than close detail will serve him best, and where, instead of a formal group, the close-up of perhaps a hand or a foot will make his most effective climax. For him, however, these will be problems of composition *ab initio* and not matters of compromise or adaptation."

The position of opera in television is in some respects similar to that of ballet. It has passed through the same phases of experiment and small-scale representation, and today it falls into the same two categories of the " television " and the " televised."

In the theatre opera has proved on the whole a more satisfactory subject for the outside broadcast camera than has ballet, largely because in most productions the full-stage picture is less vitally important in telling the story than is the individual character. Even in such works as *Nabucco*, where the whole large chorus play an essential part in the drama and are not merely commentators or living scenery, the main story lies usually in the hands of a small group. The speed at which the stage picture changes is also usually slower in opera, and this gives the camera greater opportunity for detailed exploration by travelling shots which would be quite out of place in ballet. Even so it must be admitted that spectacle as such is rarely effective on the home screen.

With the advent of bigger studios, attempts at television opera on a reasonably large scale became possible. It was very soon realized that, except in special cases, such as deliberately " period " presentations, theatre techniques must be abandoned. The main problem was visual and was the same that faced drama producers—to find a technique of story-telling in terms of close-up and medium-long, which are television's most telling shots, reserving the true long-shot only for linking and establishing general relationships. In this a very fair degree of success has been achieved, but it is still early to lay down rules as to method. Nearly every opera presents its own difficulties and requires its own individual treatment. Naturally the problems are minimized in works specially composed for the television screen. We have had an impressive number of these both in England and America, such as Menotti's *Amahl and the*

73

Night Visitors, or the pastiche operettas *Vienna Life, Paris Soir* and *A Run Away Match*, devised for the B.B.C. by James Haywood.

Curiously enough, the greatest successes to date have been among the frankly adapted theatre repertoire. Is it too wild a speculation, then, to suggest that the ultimate future of opera may lie in the studio and not in the opera house at all? There is a vast literature of fine music lying on library shelves—music which has not survived its first performances simply because the theatre of its day was technically inadequate. Once the television producer has surmounted the first hurdle and got an opera into the studio at all he can command vast resources in presentation.

In less than ten years television seems to have done something to foster the general appreciation of opera. In the theatre, the conventions of the art have always puzzled many people, some indeed have found them quite distasteful—yet on the home screen these same people have been able to accept and enjoy music drama, as the analyses of viewer reactions clearly show. Even the masque, perhaps the most difficult of all formal entertainments for the uninitiated, seems to profit by the intimacy of the screen and to have found a new home in the television studio.

The foregoing is necessarily only a sketch of television opera and the visual side of things may have been over-stressed. The entry of opera into the television studio has brought musical questions quite strange to the theatre. In the studio, for instance, the camera dictates where the singers shall be placed and may well take them right out of their familiar relationship to the orchestra and conductor. Nine times out of ten it will be quite impracticable to place the orchestra solidly in a pit between the artistes and the cameras as representing their audience. Sometimes it has even been necessary to place the instrumentalists in another studio and relay them to the singers, while the conductor has watched the action on a monitor screen—all very confusing to conventional opera artistes and a matter which music schools must now bear in mind when training future generations.

The questions of acting ability and personal appearance also become vital issues when close-up techniques are used. The actor who can sing is rare, the singer-actor rarer, yet these will

74

be more and more required, and they must be pleasant to look at even when singing all out. Films have shown this only too clearly. Interesting experiments have been made, especially in Germany, with double casts synchronized. When this does succeed it is very effective indeed but it involves quite terrible risks. In Britain, a purely mimed visual without any attempt at lip-synchronization has proved, in my view, more successful.

A large proportion of space has been given to ballet and opera because, as arts with accepted traditions, they can perhaps be the more readily and clearly discussed with reference to television. I do not want, however, to stress unduly any one side of the work.

Indeed, probably the most significant thing is that television has already developed a form of musical entertainment that is quite peculiar to itself. This, for want of a better term, is at present known as the " mixed musical." Such programmes have now reached a high state of professionalism and are typified by the extremely popular series *Music For You*. By combining elements of opera, ballet, drama, poetry and even straight concert music the creators of these programmes have, after much trial and error, reached a formula that evidently satisfies a very large proportion of the British viewing public in spite of the divergence of individual tastes.

The formula is such that its components can be kept to a high artistic standard. This has not always been the case in very popular entertainments, but it is exceedingly important in a medium which has an obviously growing impact on the cultural life of the people.

There remains to consider the place of pure concert music in television. Here is most controversial ground. There are still some who will not allow that it has any place. Music, they argue, is purely a matter for the ear and the brain—there can be no vision in it. This viewpoint cannot be wholly rejected, and, in certain branches of music, sound radio will always do all that is required. Yet the various Directors of B.B.C. Television have encouraged experiment and some quite remarkable results have appeared. Earlier it was said that music can enhance the visual experience; today there is little doubt that the converse is also true.

In this field there is still a great deal to be discovered and evaluated. At present there is only one obvious rule : that no visual matter should be grafted on to music that does not arise from it naturally, or is not powerfully suggested by it. Television has presented celebrated solo artistes, concertos with orchestra, plain orchestral concerts, even oratorio sung in the traditional manner and in nearly every case viewer reactions have justified the effort.

Sometimes it is calculated that the effect of the visual side has been small—maybe in that instance it has been ill-chosen—but sometimes it has undoubtedly been great. With the solo artiste the camera can give an intimacy unknown in the concert hall; the viewer can almost experience the singer's joy in his own song. In an orchestral concert we can learn to know the conductor as a man and not as a distant black-coated puppet; we can sit among the musicians and feel the thrill of concerted effort; or we can watch as well as listen while the composer weaves in thread after thread to complete his tapestry of sound.

In these matters there is still a vast amount to learn. Mistakes have been made, but no one will deny that the effort is well worth while.

VARIETY AND TELEVISION

MAX LIEBMAN

W HEN we began producing a series of ninety-minute *Spectaculars* for the National Broadcasting Company of the United States in September, 1954, we were moving into television territory that was not only uncharted but dangerous. No one before had had the temerity to create and produce on television what amounted to a full-fledged musical show every two weeks for nine months. Some of these were to be completely original; some would be revivals. Some would have a book; some would be revues. All of them were to be loaded with big names and given lavish production in television colour.

There were suggestions from some quarters that it could not be done. We didn't agree. We had been producing *Your Show of Shows*, a ninety-minute weekly revue starring Sid Cæsar and Imogene Coca, for five years, and we knew in advance many of the problems that might arise in producing *Spectaculars*. But we also knew that we were taking some calculated risks.

There was, for one thing, the very word *Spectacular* itself. Originally, as applied to the kind of shows which we were producing, it was merely intended to be descriptive and, considering their nature in relation to the usual run of television fare at that time, it was a reasonably apt description. But it was almost inevitable that the word should be taken as a boast on our part, the kind of boast which could scarcely be lived down by even the best of productions. If there is one thing that is pleasing, in retrospect, about our first year of producing *Spectaculars*, it is the fact that this implication of boasting is no longer inherent in the word. *Spectacular* has, in fact, become an accepted generic term without the slightest implication of a sneer.

Another problem was the fact that all our programmes would

be televised in colour, even though there were hardly any television sets in use in America at the time which could receive them in colour. This meant that we had to put in all the effort necessary to give proper production from a colour point of view even though only the merest fraction of our audience would be able to see the results of this work. Furthermore, working in colour meant moving into a huge and unfamiliar studio in Brooklyn which had just been converted for colour use (it had once been a Warner Brothers sound stage where some of the earliest Vitaphone movies were shot).

As it turned out, the necessity for working in colour proved to be a blessing in disguise. On *Your Show of Shows*, we worked on a stage and imposed on ourselves the limitations of the stage. Colour, however, gave us new leeway because it requires more space, and there was space in abundance at the Brooklyn Studio. In colour we could no longer alternate between two set-areas as we had in black-and-white. Floor colourings became as important as any other part of the set so, as a matter of necessity, most of the scenes in every production were pre-set instead of being thrown up as needed. As a result, thanks to colour, we received the unexpected opportunity of eliminating practically all scene changes while a production was on.

But these two dangers—the implications in the word *Spectacular* and the need for working in colour without a colour audience—were as nothing compared with the fact that every time we went on the air would be an opening night. There was little real continuity in either time of presentation or personnel in the shows. They were offered every fourth Saturday and every fourth Sunday with a two-week lapse between each. This is much too complicated a schedule to permit the creation of a habit pattern on the part of the public. The fact that the casts were completely different each time did not help in this matter either.

Each show was in a sense a new, fresh start and had to create its own audience. And, because it was a separate entity, we knew that we would be reviewed by the critics every time we went on the air. While the reviews have been both good and bad, the important thing is that each performance has continued to be worth the complete attention of every leading television critic in the country, which is rare in America.

As for audience continuity, a form of this has developed—a continuity not based on a time habit or the steady association of leading players, but on the acceptance of what might be called a " brand name." This provides the same kind of incentive as makes one go to see an M.G.M. picture simply because it is an M.G.M. picture, or buy Lyons' Swiss-roll because it is Lyons'.

We have been able to accomplish this because of the well-earned confidence I have in the people who work with me. Almost every member of the staff has been with me since my first day in television. We are now so accustomed to working as a team, with an intimate knowledge of the methods and thought processes of each other, that I doubt if any of us could work any other way. It is certainly only because of the existence of this organization that it is possible to put on a ninety-minute *Spectacular* every two weeks, to do a job fortnight after fortnight which would take at least three months to accomplish in the legitimate theatre.

We work on five floors of the City Centre Building in midtown New York. These floors have become so crowded by the more than two hundred people involved in the production of the shows that we have spread out to two floors of a building across the street. In these two buildings we have offices, rehearsal halls of various sizes, dressing rooms, a projection room and rooms for writers. There is an entire floor for the music department, where the music for the shows is arranged and copied, and where the shows' $750,000 collection of musical arrangements is kept. Another room contains the shows' library of nearly 200 telerecordings—complete film records of every telecast performance.

Step number one on each production is deciding on a vehicle. It might be a revival of a successful musical show—we have done *Lady in the Dark*, *Best Foot Forward*, *Babes in Toyland*, *Naughty Marietta*, *The Connecticut Yankee*, *The Merry Widow*, *The Desert Song* and *The Chocolate Soldier*—or it might be a revue built around the talents of certain stars.

In either case, our writers go to work and turn out a first draft of the script. I always work very closely with the writers and, once satisfied with the preliminary draft, a brief meeting is held with the heads of each department so that they know what will be needed.

By this time, of course, a cast has been lined up. If we are doing a revue, I usually handle the directorial work myself. For an operetta, I hire a book director. Our casts have been studded with some of the biggest names in show business—Betty Hutton, Judy Holliday, Jeanmaire, Frank Sinatra. Jimmy Durante, Sonja Henie, Jack Buchanan, the Ritz Brothers, Patrice Munsel, Alfred Drake, Perry Como, Milton Berle, Martha Raye, Ray Bolger, Eddie Albert, Janet Blair, Anne Jeffreys, Nelson Eddy, Tyrone Power and Rise Stevens are only a few of the stars who have appeared in the series.

It is in the very nature of the *Spectacular* that there should be a stress on big names, although at times I regret this. I enjoy working with highly skilled and polished talent, but one of the greatest pleasures in the past has been uncovering and giving a boost to unknowns who seemed to have the qualities of greatness. There is nothing to equal the genuine satisfaction that comes from lending a helping hand to a Danny Kaye, a Sid Cæsar or an Imogene Coca. Because established names were part of the formula for our *Spectaculars*, there has been little opportunity to provide a showcasing for promising unknowns in this series, although I was able to introduce to the American television audience the French comedian, Jacques Tati, and Britain's Jean Carson (who is called Jeannie Carson in the States to avoid confusion with an American actress named Jean Carson).

Once the first draft of the script is finished and the cast is set, we have two weeks in which to produce a programme within the necessary budget limitations (each of our productions usually costs in the neighbourhood of $300,000, including air time). Beginning on Monday of the first week, our five floors in the City Centre Building are alive with arrangers, copyists, script-writers, prop men and members of the cast—writing, listening, building, rehearsing. Across the street in "The Annex," dancers are learning their routines under the guidance of Rod Alexander who, with his wife Bambi Linn, has the featured dancing role in most of our productions. On the floor above the dancers, Clay Warnick is rehearsing the singers.

A few blocks away our costume designer, Paul du Pont, has an office at the Eaves Costume Company, where his two assistants, along with forty dressmakers and twenty tailors, are cutting and stitching costumes. Farther downtown, in a big creaky old building on 23rd Street, Frederick Fox and a staff of ten scenic artists build and paint the sets.

It is particularly in the work of du Pont and Fox that this matter of having confidence in one's staff is evident. It means that, once I have seen their sketches and know whether or not they have caught what I have in mind, I also know that they will carry them out from there exactly as wanted.

While each member of the staff is hard at work concentrating on his particular area of the job, I am on the move from one rehearsal to another—from singing rehearsal to dancing rehearsal to script rehearsal. During this first week of rehearsal, there are two production meetings at night at which progress and problems are discussed.

In addition to guiding the work on the show which is in rehearsal, we are preparing for the production which will follow, looking at sketches of costumes and sets for the future, holding meetings on music and choreography, negotiating contracts with stars, auditioning new people, consulting with executives of the National Broadcasting Company about advertising and promotion of our productions, and checking kinescopes of past productions in a continuing search for methods of improvement.

After rehearsing for a week and a half, we have the first complete run-through. Now, for the first time, we really see in proper perspective what we have been doing for the past ten days. From this run-through we get the clues for the necessary cutting and polishing.

The next day we move into the studio—to the colour studio in Brooklyn for a book show or to the Colonial Theatre on upper Broadway for a revue. The revues are done in the theatre because we have found that the response of an audience is an essential ingredient for their success. We have no audience in the Brooklyn Studio.

Our last three days before going on the air are spent either in the studio or the theatre. There my associate producer-director, Bill Hobin, blocks out the camera angles. The cast rehearses in costume for the first time, works with the orchestra for the first time and gets used to the sets. At this point we are joined by thirty-four crew members from the National Broadcasting Company—technicians such as cameramen, video

F

men, audiomen, boom-operators, dolly pushers, cablemen, colour consultants and other specialists.

Finally it is Saturday (or Sunday, as the case may be). The results of our two weeks of concentrated rehearsal appear on millions of black-and-white television sets and a few hundred colour ones, and then, almost as soon as we fade off the screen, rehearsals are started on the next *Spectacular*. This continues seven days a week for ten months of the year.

TELEVISION FOR CHILDREN

MICHAEL WESTMORE

NOT so many years ago children's entertainment was an easy-going, haphazard affair. Indeed, the days when children were rarely seen and hardly ever heard are within human memory. Entertainment of any sort was still suspect. It concerned Papa and Uncle Arthur (with one or two riotous friends) going out on a rather carefully undefined spree which took in a music-hall at some time during the evening— or it might be a matinée which Mama attended now and then in a new hat. It never invaded the nursery—apart from an excursion to a Christmas pantomime or circus and Punch-and-Judy on the beach.

It is difficult to fix the exact date when the attitude to children changed—though it may well have coincided with the breakdown of the strictly-ordered family life that followed the First World War and it happened at about the same time that entertainment began to be almost respectable. Already Arthur Mee had brought out in monthly instalments his *Children's Encyclopædia*; already Baden-Powell's Boy Scouts had pedalled round whistling and bugling to signal the approach of the Zeppelin; and in the mid-twenties there came, through the trumpet-shaped loudspeaker of the wireless, a regular hour for children every day of the week.

This was, on a small scale, a social revolution. Parents suffered a rebuff from which they have never recovered. Before radio they were to their children the interpreters of the world and the unquestioned arbiters of taste. Now, no sooner was the childish ear ready to receive and understand than it was monopolized for a solid hour by a body of experts whose fund of stories and information, plays and music, was bound to put father and mother in the shade. The piano in the parlour was not tuned so often and the pages of the *Student's Song Book* began to moulder in the attic.

Now, another war has bellowed, blasted and whimpered to a standstill and television has invaded millions of homes. Every day children in ones, twos and threes sit glued to a set. However discerning and sensible their parents may be the plain fact is that children see, one way and another, a great deal of television. This places the people behind the sets—in the studios— in a position of great responsibility because, however unimportant the individual programme may seem to them, the impact on their audience is tremendous and the possible results incalculable. I say "however unimportant" because, in the hurlyburly of television production, it is sometimes very difficult to remember these facts. For people working in television the fact that the programme goes on at all is often such a miracle that the end product is forgotten. I do not defend this state of affairs but must recognize its existence.

The trouble about television is that it never stops, and therefore the times when a producer or director can sit back and think what he is doing are few and far between. It follows that he must be so versed in the technique of production that this becomes second nature to him. Until this is so his contribution to programmes, however great his capabilities, can be little more than pedestrian. He is, to his colleagues, a nuisance and to his audience—a bore. This is true of television, whether it be for adults or for children.

Producing television programmes for children has, of course, problems of its own. It is the newest branch of the newest type of entertainment and so, inevitably, in recruiting people to write for it, direct for it and appear in it there must be much experiment and much failure. Humour is a case in point. As most amateur and professional comedians know to their cost, the joke that convulses the saloon-bar may fall very flat in the drawing-room. Equally a visual gag that has stood the test of hundreds of pantomime seasons may not so much as dimple the cheek of one little girl sitting by herself in front of a television receiver.

For comedy must be scaled to the size and character of its audience. A circus clown means very little on television be-

84

cause he is used to playing in a hollow O surrounded by audiences that build him from gag to gag with great gusts of laughter. Confronted by a camera in the sticky silence of a television studio he is lost and gone for ever. One answer to this problem—the problem of giving a comedian something pliable to work on—is the studio audience. These people can be infuriating to the home-viewers because their laughs are nearly always based on some reaction or " business " which they can see and the viewer cannot. But, with all their faults, they at least provide the performer with some evidence that he is not working to the empty air and two disillusioned and deadpan cameramen.

In children's programmes, however, the studio audience is virtually impossible if it is to be of children. It is difficult enough to meet laws, by-laws and fire regulations and so get children performing in British television studios at all; to provide an audience of children without breaking several regulations is almost as precarious an undertaking as transporting a school of porpoises to the centre of the Sahara.

This means that the comedian can never know, except by hearsay, his impact on his audience—and hearsay is of very little help when it is concerned with something like the correct timing of comedy material. He must rely entirely on his own sense of timing and his experience and upon the advice of his producer. In the circumstances when a comedian, well liked and well established in other media, fails to amuse it is perhaps fair to remember the magnitude of the task he has set himself.

Another problem, mentioned in passing above, is having children in the studio at all, whether they are amateur or professional. Shirley Temple, Freddie Bartholomew, Bobbie Henrey could not have appeared on a British television screen (in a live performance) until they had reached the magic age of twelve. At that age they would have been so encumbered by regulations as to the length of rehearsal time allowed that their final performance would have been a haphazard and risky business.

Amateur children are bound by very much the same rules. A programme like *All Your Own*, in which appear children who do anything interesting from bee-keeping to ballet-dancing, has achieved great success, but, because of these regulations, it has always had to pretend that childhood begins at twelve years old.

None of the interesting pursuits of "real children" can be featured at all.

While granting that young children should not be exploited and that every care should be taken to protect them, it is still a tragedy that this "window on the world" is permitted to show so little of the golden age of childhood. At twelve years old children are beginning to be young adults, and there are few things so embarrassing as seeing a small fourteen-year-old performing the part of a child of eight in a play. This is a very real problem in presenting television programmes for children.

It is interesting to reflect how complicated it is, because of this ruling, to present the great classics that appeal particularly to children. There is a considerable risk of a patchy performance by under-rehearsed child actors if stories with a number of children, or a child in a principal part, are undertaken. *David Copperfield* and *Oliver Twist* must remain, literally, on the shelf.

This is a pity because there is no doubt that serialized versions of the classics have a great attraction. In answer to the objection that this is spoon-feeding, it is fair to recall that the greater part of Dickens' writing, for example, came out originally in weekly instalments. It is also fair to admit that even to many adults there is a formidable quality about some of the works of Dickens, Thackeray and Scott, and that, unless one is convinced that there is something worth finding in the vast and unknown interior of the books, one may not survive the first fifty pages. Television serials can help young readers to climb that rather dreary path and see the glory of the valley beyond.

People often say that this method of presenting great literature will prevent children reading at all. Such a distinguished and disinterested journal as *The Times Educational Supplement* contested this view when it reported that whenever excerpts from the classics were presented on television there was, following the transmission, a much increased demand for the particular books at public libraries. So that, despite dire warnings from some quarters of the terrible effect television has on children, it is possible to combine enlightenment with entertainment.

But it is difficult to achieve a proper balance between enlightenment and entertainment, if indeed the two territories can be always distinguished. For it is a peculiarity of television that a pair of hands embroidering may be more "entertaining" than a juggling act. But in so far as they can be divided, there is a clear obligation upon those who control this compelling machine to ensure that its power for enlightenment is always uppermost in their minds. In this respect it is well to remember that, while children will laugh and play without the aid of television, they cannot have access without it to so many things that it can provide. Documentary features and news items are not outside children's comprehension, and help to satisfy, for a brief moment, their insatiable and natural curiosity.

Showing children how to make things for themselves is another positive and valuable function of television. Children have creative and destructive impulses; this medium can do much to encourage the creative impulse by showing how to make something, but, more important still, by showing that other children have managed to bring it off. It is easy to remember the sense of frustration in childhood when two pieces of wood just would not stay together or paint would run and spoil the outlines of a painting. Television can help here enormously by sharing out these problems. "The man on the screen has shown me how to do it. I've tried and failed, but he is showing me an example from another child who has succeeded. It can be done. Directly the programme is over I am going to dash off and have another go."

So that, far from encouraging docility and uniformity in children, television promotes the exercise of their minds and their bodies. It suggests new hobbies that might otherwise never have come within their sphere of knowledge. It leads the way toward books and paintings that can supersede the pile of " comics " and special adaptations for children. It enables them to see the best that can be shown of the world of sport. It crosses frontiers and enables them to see that the children, and even the grown-ups, of other countries are human beings.

Above all, in a country of small families, it means that they can share their pleasures with a vast new family of friendly contemporaries.

THE TELEVISION NEWSREEL

THE taste of audiences for television, as for any form of entertainment, varies greatly; but about one television programme in Britain at least opinions have never been divided—news is popular with everyone.

In pre-war days the B.B.C. Television Service used to show the Gaumont and British Movietone cinema newsreels. It was hoped, when the service reopened in June, 1946 (after the wartime blackout), that not only these two reels but the other three British newsreels would be available for television in rotation. This, however, was not to be; the British film industry saw in television a competitor.

The B.B.C. therefore decided to expand its small existing Television Film Unit and to produce its own newsreel specially for the television service. Preliminary work began during the autumn of 1947, and on January 5th, 1948, the first edition of what was to become the most popular of all television's regular programmes, *Television Newsreel*, was transmitted.

Technically it was crude; and it suffered, too, by reason of its birth-date. Real news of a pictorial nature is usually scarce at the turn of the year, and weather conditions seldom favour good photography. Nevertheless, *Television Newsreel* was an immediate success. With the start of the winter Olympic Games in Switzerland at the end of the month it was increased from one to two editions a week. Its length was nearly fifteen minutes—twice the length of commercial cinema newsreels—and it soon became apparent that in this added length it had a great advantage over its commercial counterparts, not only because the additional time allowed for the inclusion of more

88

" stories " but also because it permitted each item to run for a greater length, to be developed more fully and at a slower tempo, since it was found that the home screen was unsuited to the faster style of the cinema.

With the right formula becoming clear, technical quality was improved. The staff settled down to work as an efficient team, better equipment became available, and at the end of 1950 the two weekly editions were increased to three, and then to five in June, 1952, at which frequency it remained until it was taken over by the B.B.C.'s News Division in July, 1954. From this time onward, the presentation of what was called *News and Newsreel* ceased to be a direct responsibility of the Television Service, although technicians and some other staff were seconded to the News Division of B.B.C.'s sound radio. The production process used today for the presentation differs, of course, from that built up for *Television Newsreel*.

Apart from its greater length and frequency of issue, *Television Newsreel* differed from the commercial reels in another very important respect. It was, of course, a newsreel, and as such produced entirely on film. The subjects chosen for inclusion, therefore, were selected as much for their pictorial as for their news value; we were not at that time attempting to put out anything in the nature of a news bulletin. But while the commercial reels were faced with a time-lag of at least two days before the pictures taken by their cameramen could appear on the screen (during which time the film had to be edited, a commentary recorded and up to four hundred copies printed and distributed throughout the country), the B.B.C. was able to show the film within a few hours of its reaching the laboratories. There were no prints to make, no problems of distributing them over the country, and the commentary could be recorded on magnetic tape a few minutes before transmission— or even, if necessary, spoken live as the film itself was transmitted. It was inevitable that, without any special effort on the B.B.C.'s part, *Television Newsreel* should be more topical, more up-to-date than its film trade rivals.

Before discussing in detail the functions of each member of the production team, it might be useful to give a brief description of the production process in general.

Every morning a meeting was held in the Newsreel Manager's office, attended by the producer, the planning assistant on duty

89

and the editorial assistant. The latter was responsible for watching the newspapers and for seeing that no important forthcoming item of news was overlooked. At this meeting suggestions for stories were discussed, sorted out, accepted, rejected, or if not of an immediate topical character filed away as future "possibles." These suggestions came from many sources—from those present at the meeting, from the News Room at Broadcasting House, from the organizers of public functions and from viewers themselves. At this daily meeting the contents of that day's edition was decided and the main items for coverage during the next few days entered in the diary.

Meanwhile film from cameramen out in the field would be reaching the laboratories. After development, it came to the cutting-rooms where, under the supervision of the producer, the various scenes were edited into correct sequence. As soon as a story had been edited and approved by the producer, a list was made out showing the sequence of shots and the exact length of each as a guide to the writer in preparing the commentary. Normally, by six o'clock in the evening, all stories had been edited and provided with commentaries; sound tracks of effects noises and suitable music had also been added.

The producer's task was now to record the latter on to one magnetic track ready for transmission. This was done in the dubbing theatre, which is equipped with film projectors, gramophone turntables, microphones and control panels. On one side of a glass-paned division Edward Halliday, for so long the voice of *Television Newsreel*, read the prepared script. He may have been accompanied by a guest commentator—perhaps Charles Gardiner if there was an air story, or Barbara Mandel to speak a piece on women's fashions. In the adjoining control-room the producer and sound-recordists mixed in the train and aeroplane noises, the music and the sound of marching feet, or whatever other effects were appropriate. Time for a run through in the projection theatre, and then another edition of *Television Newsreel* was ready to go on the air.

To achieve a screen-time of just under fifteen minutes a day for five days each week, a team of some thirty people was necessary. Those of whose work the public is most conscious are, of course, the cameramen. The life of a newsreel cameraman is a hard one; one which he can never call his own. In theory, B.B.C. cameramen do a five-day working week, but even on their rest days they are never free from the rest-shattering telephone call directing them to the scene of some railway crash or fire. Such lost rest days are naturally made up to them at a later date and invariably accepted with cheerfulness.

But the man who likes his life to run to a well-ordered routine had better seek his living in an office or bank. As a newsreel cameraman he will probably find that, having spent the day on the spray-swept deck of a tug in heavy weather off the South Foreland, he returns tired out at night only to learn that there has been an earthquake in Greece and that he has just two hours in which to catch the night plane for Athens.

If he can take this kind of irregular life, what qualities must he possess? Competency as a cine-photographer, of course, but more than that; he must be something also of a journalist and reporter. There are no shooting-scripts for newsreel work. The cameraman must be able to tell the story—the whole story —with his pictures, shooting all the time " off the cuff " with nothing to guide him except his own news-sense. His film must tell us " where," " how " and sometimes " why." Clever editing has salvaged many a poor piece of camera-work but at the expense of much time and worry. There is no room in a newsreel unit for a cameraman who thinks that as long as there is a picture of sorts on the film it is enough.

Whenever possible, newsreel stories are shot with what is called " live sound "—that is, speech or background noises recorded on the spot. On these occasions a sound-recordist accompanies the cameraman, whose life and conditions he shares. Working alone, the cameraman uses a small hand-camera, but for sound recording a larger camera, mounted on a tripod, is employed. This records the sound on the same film as the picture. This single-system method, as it is called, is the responsibility of the recordist. The latter must have a good ear and be fully versed in the workings and problems of low-frequency amplifiers, microphones, oscillographs and acoustics. It is his job to see that the microphone is correctly placed (sometimes there are several) and throughout the run he monitors the sound at a control panel to ensure that it is recorded at the correct level on the film.

Sometimes, however, because of shortage of equipment or for other reasons it is not practicable to record sound on the spot.

In *Television Newsreel* the deficiency was remedied by selecting appropriate sound effects tracks from the sound film library and arranging these to synchronize with the pictures. The greatest care was exercised in the choice of these sound tracks, yet there was an occasional slip. A viewer once wrote to complain that the sound he had heard as Geoff Duke's Norton passed the camera in the T.T. race in the Isle of Man was in fact the exhaust note of another (and very similar) make of machine. He was right.

Opinions are divided on the ethics of adding " library " sound to newsreel film. One school of thought declares it to be wrong and deceitful. This is no doubt true where a false impression might be given—an unpopular public figure, for example, apparently received with loud cheering when in fact he was greeted with mute disapproval—but surely there is something ridiculous in the spectacle of a cavalcade of tanks moving down the road in complete silence?

The third link in the production chain as the newsreel passes on its way to the screen was the film editor—or editors, since there were several on duty each day. Their task was to view the film as it was received from the laboratories after processing and, in collaboration with the producer, to decide how much screen time each item was worth. In the cutting-rooms the rolls of film, known as " rushes," are cut up and separated into individual shots. *Television Newsreel* was largely projected as negative for transmission over television. The editors had to accustom themselves to recognizing people and places in this form—no easy task as those who have watched the B.B.C.'s *Puzzle Corner* programmes will realize. With the aid of an editing machine, which is a type of small film projector, the shots were matched, shortened and joined in correct sequence to the length allotted to the story. The editors were guided by the cameraman's " dope-sheet "—a list and description of each shot which he should write down (and often does not!) at the time of shooting—and their task was to arrange the various pieces of film in the best possible way to tell the story clearly and in the right sequence.

Much experience is needed to become an efficient film editor —a shot in the wrong place and the smooth running of the story may be completely lost. The work, moreover, must be carried out at high speed, with an impatient commentary writer waiting in the background to take over his part of the operation.

When *Television Newsreel* started in 1948 Edward Halliday used both to write and speak the commentary, but the increasing number of editions each week made the task too much for one man. A staff of three writers was eventually needed. These viewed the stories as soon as picture editing had been completed (they collaborated with the editor on some occasions) and then, working from the short list made previously, saw that their written commentaries synchronized exactly with the film as edited.

Apart from a wide knowledge of current affairs, considerable experience is needed to provide a good newsreel commentary. It is useless and, indeed, annoying to viewers to describe in words what they can see for themselves. The commentary should fill in the gaps left by the pictures, add the background, identify people—and no more. Frequently, pictures are best left to tell the story without any commentary at all. A good commentary writer should know when to talk and when to keep quiet. To aid them in their work they have firstly the cameraman's dope-sheet, supported by newspaper cuttings and books of reference, and most important of all the telephone. Facts and figures cannot be taken for granted; they must be checked and rechecked until no doubt remains as to their correctness. The B.B.C. has a reputation for accuracy which must be preserved.

These then are the technicians whose work reached the screen in tangible form, as it were. But behind them were others—the producers who were responsible for the way the final product was presented on the screen and the planning assistants whose task was to pave the way for the cameramen. They drew up the cameraman's instructions for each assignment, arranged for the necessary permits and press passes, found out if special lighting would be required and if so what the voltage was of the local electricity mains supply, ascertained whether the film, if sent back by train, would reach the laboratories in time or, if not, whether there was a scheduled air-service which would serve, and arranged the multitude of details without whose smooth working the newsreel service could not function.

What of the future? There can be little doubt that in television news the live component will play an ever-increasing

93

part. By this is meant, not the introduction of studio speakers and interviews, but outside broadcasts direct from the scene showing viewers the news as it is actually happening. The B.B.C.'s new Roving Eye equipment has already freed television (as opposed to film) cameras from the tangle of cables which formerly tied them to a fixed and restricted base. Britain is now joined by a permanent radio-television link to the continent of Europe; one day, perhaps, a similar link may be established with North America.

Few news items, of course, are ever likely to happen during the actual time that a newsreel is scheduled for transmission, but the advantages are very great of televising them back to base as they occur and recording the pictures on film for use later in the day; the problems of transport vanish. The recording of commentary can thus be left until the last possible moment and a completely up-to-date account of the situation presented. A start has already been made in this direction. The technique may be developed greatly in the near future. There is no doubt that news in television offers a very exciting future.

ACTING IN TELEVISION

JOAN MILLER

T HE actor's successful existence depends on the numbers and enthusiasm of his audience, wherever they may be. Having played to full houses in a theatre seating one thousand, eight times a week for a year, an actor will have been seen by only one twenty-fifth of the number of people who potentially could watch him give a single performance in a television production. The B.B.C. estimates its average maximum audience is 11 million,* but that is not to say that the average drama production achieves this number of viewers. For this reason alone the question of television acting is vital to all professional actors. Already the popularity of the new medium is phenomenal.

Just as the growth of the film industry was at first catastrophic for the legitimate theatre, so this latest and even more powerful rival is dealing both theatre and cinema a further crippling blow. Actors can look forward to a near future when the bulk of available opportunity for expression, career and livelihood will come from television. This forecast is self-evident and it poses a problem for the future of all stage, screen and television performers.

A theatre training has always been deemed essential to the actor regardless of what other fields he may choose to specialize in later. Owing, however, to the increasing popularity of television, support for the live theatre has drastically decreased and repertory companies and the small experimental theatres, which have always provided initial experience for our future actors and have frequently produced a consistently high standard, are closing down all over Britain. There appears to be no

* This was prior to the starting of commercial television.

alternative training ground. Drama schools offer few of the benefits which derive from practical experience. This situation cannot be ignored.

Actors who have worked exclusively and successfully in the theatre are sometimes inclined to patronize their more famous and highly-paid fellow artistes in the film industry, but if workers in either branch of entertainment wish to attain success as television artistes they decry each other's media at their peril. It is true that many good stage actors have become equally good film actors. It is also true that it is almost unknown for a film actor, no matter how distinguished, to achieve success in the theatre unless he has had a stage background. When acting on television, however, artistes without exception use every grain of experience gathered in film studio and theatre because demands are made upon them which they have not hitherto met.

The requirements of television acting seem to have brought about, at last, a marriage of sorts between the stage and screen. Perhaps, in the future, a method of acting entirely peculiar to the new medium will emerge—the D. W. Griffith and the Chaplin of television have yet to be discovered—but in the meantime a blend of qualities, some stemming from the stage and some from film experience, plus certain basic qualities which are essential to both, go to make up good television acting at the present time.

Concentration, sincerity and relaxation are all three necessary attributes of good acting in any medium. Command over them is required to the greatest possible degree in television where the resources of the most highly-experienced actors are taxed to the utmost.

Both stage and television actors must be able to memorize easily and accurately. Such concentrated study is not necessary for filming because only short sequences are shot at a time. A screen actor has also the comfort of knowing that if he does forget his lines the scene can be taken again, although lapses of memory certainly do not add to his popularity with the director. On the stage, in an emergency, a "dry" or a "fluff" can be easily covered. Actors know a dozen ways of helping each other or covering their own mistakes and the audience is seldom any the wiser. When playing for television this is not possible. I have never yet seen an actor "dry" without it being painfully and embarrassingly noticeable. The illusion, which should be preserved at all costs, is lost and often not regained. So, "being a good study" is of paramount importance to a television actor.

Stage and television actors must be able to sustain long and demanding parts both mentally and emotionally. On the stage an actor, safe behind his "fourth wall," can bring all his art and experience to bear on creating and recreating the character he has so carefully built up during rehearsal. The audience, whose contact he loves, is there, but comfortably cut off from him. The conditions back-stage are designed to help him to concentrate, to relive his part night after night. There is always at least one interval, when he alters his make-up, does his elaborate changes, rests for a moment. And there is still, in the theatre, an atmosphere of consideration and appreciation from the stage door-keeper, the dressers, stage-hands, stage staff—in fact, everyone bred of the theatre, which fosters the idea, for a few hours each night, that what is taking place is special and important. This, of course, is infinitely precious to the actor who must be constantly reassured that the "make-believe" he creates is important. It is only in the legitimate theatre that he will receive this sort of understanding.

As the stage door closes behind him, he must realize he is in a different world; a world of mechanized entertainment where technicians are really more important than the actor. He can no longer indulge in his romantic "horse-and-carriage" ideas —the ideas of the theatre—in the world of the film and of the new medium, television.

To sustain a long part in a television production is a very different matter from performing the same part in the theatre. The actor's concentration must be much more controlled because he must enact a role, often in constrained floor-space where there should be ample stage-space, with three, four or even five cameras moving in and out, often in front of his very nose. At times the particular camera to which he is playing can break down before his eyes and another camera take over at an angle unfavourable to the actor, but he must go on acting, showing no sign that he is anything but composed and completely master of the situation.

All scene waits and most act waits are, of course, cut out in television scripts, forcing the actor to perform his changes of costume and make-up at break-neck speed. Sometimes he may have to dash from one set to another for different scenes which have to be played with calm and dignity, deep anguish, or lighthearted gaiety—none of which moods is within a thousand miles of the sweating, distraught player. But he must not turn a hair; the illusion must never be shattered for the vast audience of viewers. He can only hope that the sweat pouring down his brow will not be picked up on the screen. What would Stanislavsky have thought if he had known what demands would be made on actors so shortly after he gave his " method " of acting to the world of the theatre?

Contact with the public is always a source of enjoyment to an actor, and as he becomes more and more experienced he learns to " handle " various types of audiences. They can be as divergent in their behaviour and reaction as individuals, and the power he comes to wield over them gives him great satisfaction. In a television production, as in film-making, the actor has none of the pleasure and inspiration of personal contact, but he experiences to the full that nervous apprehension and emotion which are always strongly ingrained in all actors. In television this reaction is more concentrated because the audience numbers millions of viewers and the actor has only this one opportunity to put his performance " over." Millions of eyes are fixed on him, millions of ears are listening, but the effect he is making cannot be gauged at that same moment as in the theatre; he has little notion whether they think well or ill of him. Somehow those millions of viewers are symbolized by the merciless eye of the television camera which is recording every nervous twitch, every flicker of an eyelash, every bead of sweat—and most frightening of all—every thought. It is because of this electronic camera that the actor feels gratitude for each moment of previous film experience for, as far as actual method is concerned, the television actor must follow the film actor very closely indeed.

Both film and television actors find that, for the sake of the camera, physical movement must be rigidly controlled by the director. The artist must accustom himself to walk from one marked spot on the set to another with absolute accuracy, never indicating that the movement is not completely spontaneous and free. He must largely abandon the sense of theatrical reality which he works so hard to master inside the framework of the make-believe of the theatre and yet, paradoxically, a much greater degree of naturalness is required for either type of photographed performance than would be necessary on the stage.

A highly-developed imagination, another constantly sought-after faculty in all actors, should be at his command because he must be able to convince an audience of a situation in which he has no possibility of convincing himself. An example may be that he must deliver an impassioned love speech in close-up. Because of the camera, far from gazing into the eyes of his beloved as he pours forth his heart, he is possibly staring at a technician's hand which is being held up to give him his " eye line."

Actors in both the film and television mediums must play with absolute sincerity and naturalness. There must be no hint of unreality. To be able " to project " is one of the greatest of a stage actor's assets. Self-projection means heightening, enlarging, both vocally and physically and, although the result must appear natural to the audience in the theatre, it is in fact larger than life. This technique must be put aside in a film or television studio. Indeed, almost all film directors think it infinitely preferable if it has never been learnt, and it is because of this quality in stage actors that they are less welcome in film studios than artistes trained especially for a camera technique.

Both film and television actors must be able to convey thought and emotion with a minimum of facial expression. Facial mannerisms which pass unnoticed in the theatre become unsightly and grotesque through the camera's eye. Just as sustaining a long part without any breaks presents a big problem to a film actor, so acting in what at first feels like a straight-jacket—that is, with an immobile face—seems impossible to the stage actor. Later, as he learns to convey a feeling with no facial expression at all except the eyes, and that often without any movement of the eye, the actor begins to feel something of his old sense of satisfaction. On the stage, to express a point, an actor might use his entire body in a movement; his hands, a turn of his head, the use of eyes and mouth. At first it seems impossible that, because of the magnifying effect of the camera, exactly the same result can be achieved, and must be achieved, with no movement of any kind.

Finally, the quality of teamwork between actors is as necessary to a television production as it is to a theatrical presentation. Interplay and reaction among players is largely the result of the director's skilful management. In films it depends to a great extent on expert editing.

Really successful television plays, at the moment of writing, are those which can be photographed for the most part in close-up, or close shots of small groups of actors. The player's reactions are of tremendous importance. This is one of the many reasons which are likely to bring about an alternative type of presentation to the live performance.

During the months of preparation for a commercial television service in Britain a method of play production was used which could be infinitely superior to the live method, combining the virtues of both stage and screen to get a satisfactory result. A play of one hour's duration is rehearsed for ten days in the same manner as a stage production as far as the actors are concerned. As a result they attain a first-night standard before they reach the studio floor. They are word-perfect, they know not only their own parts but the play as a whole, and they are able to perform their entire parts with the same overall conception they would give to a stage production. It is of vital importance that the director should have a background of stage or television experience so that the rehearsal period can be utilized to the full. At the end of ten days the play is ready to go " on the floor." It is then filmed in three or four days, using the technique of a television production.

By this method full profit is derived from the rehearsal period in that the actors, although working as film players, will know as much about the play as a whole as they would in the theatre and will be able to sustain long "takes" of ten or more minutes. Added to this advantage are the benefits attaching to a film production: each scene can be expertly lit and photographed and it can be edited and cut on completion. If a shot is unsatisfactory it can be taken again. There is none of the " do or die " atmosphere of the live television production, glamorous as it may be. The director, actors and technicians know what they are doing and have the opportunity to recify mistakes.

For current events, parlour games, personality spots and even variety shows the all too often " off the cuff " result of live television need not necessarily do irreparable damage, but, for television drama production to reach a high level, some method of presentation should be used whereby the result will not be haphazard and where the hard-won qualities and experience of the expert actor can be utilized.

STUDIOS AND SERVICES

ORGANIZATION AND PLANNING

ROBIN WHITWORTH

THE B.B.C. Television Service comprises seven main programme producing departments concerned with drama, music, light entertainment, talks, outside broadcasts and special programmes for women and children. These programme or " output " departments, which consist of producers, production assistants and secretaries, are supported not only by the engineering and the technical staff but also by five main service departments. These are concerned with the booking of artistes, provision of film sequences, design and supply of scenery and " props," the making-up and dressing of performers and the mounting and presentation of programmes in the studios or elsewhere. The work of them all is co-ordinated by a small central Planning Unit.

Each programme department has a Head and an Organizer. The latter's main duties are to ensure the proper arrangement of the work of producers and the smooth and efficient provision of all necessary materials and facilities, to prepare estimates and control expenditure and assist the Head of his department with all aspects of programme and staff administration. The organizer also acts on behalf of the Planning Unit in helping to integrate the work of his own department with the activities and output of the service as a whole.

The organizer is first concerned with the mounting of a production at the time when advance schedules of programmes are made up. Some programmes may be mounted at very short notice: others may need months of preparation. The plan of each day's programme output must thus be made up sufficiently far in advance to ensure that the most complicated documentary programme, for example, can be ready in time;

and yet it must be left sufficiently flexible for the inclusion of topical items nearer to and even on the day of transmission itself. The people concerned with planning must also be sure well beforehand that the necessary studios, camera-crews, filming and scenery-building effort and all other facilities will be available for all the programmes that are envisaged. An advance schedule may cover a period of from three to six months and must be ready at least eight weeks before the period starts.

Programme ideas come from producers, Heads of departments and other officials, and often from viewers themselves—in fact, from anyone. To be adopted, an idea must reach a producer who will handle it with enthusiasm, and it must fit into the pattern of programme output as a whole. Ideas are discussed first between producers and the Head of their department, and then between the departmental Heads and the Controller of Programmes. When lists of programmes are thus prepared according to an agreed pattern, it is for the Planning Unit and the organizers to ensure that these plans are feasible.

Television anywhere in the world has to work with limited resources in terms of studios, equipment, preparatory effort and money. Organizers must thus discuss with every producer exactly what each of his proposed programmes will involve. How much rehearsal will be necessary? How large a cast? How much scenery, what music and what special effects? Will some of the scenes have to be filmed, and if so, how many days shooting and how much editing will be necessary? Will any such filming be located at home or abroad? Will any foreign currency be required? And how much will it all cost?

There are a myriad questions to be asked and answered, and widely varied points to be watched. If children of between twelve and fifteen years old are to be included in the cast, regulations in Britain require that they shall leave the studio by ten o'clock, so the time of the transmission must be fixed accordingly. A certain studio may be essential for some particular programme on account of its size or technical equipment. A programme may be tied to a definite week or day on account of some occasion or the availability of artistes. It is by considerations such as these that the preliminary plans for each department's programmes are conditioned.

There are many difficulties at this stage. The efficient employment of producers will depend on the acceptance or rejec-

106

tion of their suggestions, which often cannot be finally decided until they are viewed in relation to the suggestions put forward by all other London departments and the Regions of the B.B.C. Uncertainty as to the availability of particular artistes several months ahead may make it impossible to decide the date of a play or the order in which various Light Entertainment programmes or series can be fixed. The dates of important sporting events may not be known. A producer may not be able to provide sufficient information about the requirements of a play or documentary programme, the script of which is not yet written.

In cases of doubt, an organizer must guess to the best of his ability in the light of his experience. He makes up a draft schedule of the programmes offered by his department, with the fullest possible indication of the resources and facilities required, based on a mixture of fact and foresight. He then discusses his department's proposals with the Head of the Programme Planning unit, who in turn will correlate the proposals and requirements of all London departments and the Regions and trim them, in consultation with the Controller of Programmes, in relation to the resources and facilities available. Finally he issues the schedule of programmes for a three- or six-monthly period to which all departments must work.

Eight weeks in advance of transmissions the organizers of each department meet with the Head of the Planning Unit and the representatives of all the service departments to review the projected arrangements for the week two months' ahead. The provision of scenery is considered: more " effort " is often required than is available and adjustments have to be made. Changes in the schedule are made to incorporate items that have just become available; programmes that have failed to materialize are replaced. The arrangements for filming, wardrobe and make-up, and the means of overcoming all kinds of financial and operational difficulties are reviewed. Then the plans for the programmes in the week in question are agreed.

From now on the organizer must watch the cost of the programmes being prepared by his department. It is often difficult to know how much has been or is being spent, particularly if there is filming abroad. Estimates can be carefully prepared, but when the time comes costs may be increased by transport or customs problems or by delays in shooting because of bad weather. The exact total cost of a programme may not be known until two or three weeks after its transmission. If one programme costs less than expected, more money is available for others; if another programme costs too much, savings must be found elsewhere. The organizer must ensure that his periodic allocation is not exceeded.

Meanwhile other problems arise. The organizer may have to advise a producer about casting, or help him to get more rehearsal or film servicing or special equipment than he originally thought he would require. There are *Radio Times* and other publicity statements to be checked; perhaps the photographing of artistes or scenery to be arranged, and hospitality to be provided for leading performers, distinguished visitors and people who may have helped with the preparation of a programme.

All the time there is business to be done connected with the administration of programmes and staff. There is correspondence with people who put forward ideas for programmes or want to write scripts; there may be letters of appreciation or protest to be dealt with after a programme has been transmitted; there is the assessment of fees for scripts and performances. Staff administration involves checking claims for the repayment of expenses, recording sick-leave and preparation of annual holiday rotas to suit the wishes of individuals without hindering output; submitting cases for bonuses and extra duty pay, and making some of the arrangements for recruitment and training of staff, whether for permanent appointment or for holiday relief.

Organizers are also concerned with the arrangements made with British Actors' Equity, the Musicians' Union, the Performing Rights Society and other bodies which watch the interests of performers and the many different people who contribute in various ways to the programmes. There are many such agreements covering hours of work and rates of payment, the use of music, both live and recorded, the various uses to which film sequences or telerecordings of complete programmes may or may not be put and so on. Organizers must ensure that all the conditions in all such agreements are observed and provide information relevant to their re-negotiation as circumstances and requirements change from time to time.

There are also questions concerning the type of new equipment that should be installed in the studios and the ways in which production and technical staff may best co-operate. Such matters are discussed at regular meetings held every fortnight between departmental organizers and senior engineers. There may, for instance, be much discussion as to what types of dolly are most suitable for the mounting and movement of cameras. Or the engineers may wish to know how much some facility, such as back-projection of scenery or telecine machines for the showing of film, is likely to be required by producers in coming months, so that they can decide whether additional staff will be needed for double-shift working. They might wish to discuss whether camera-crews should specialize in particular types of production, or be allocated to every type of programme from time to time. Any question concerning co-operation between programme staff and engineers may be raised at these meetings. Smooth co-operation between programme and technical staff is of prime importance to the success of the television undertaking.

Organizers are thus jacks-of-many-trades. No organizer can be completely the master of every aspect of his work, which ranges from the laws of copyright to finance and from questions of artistic judgment to the intricacies of electronic equipment: but every organizer must master the essentials of the various trades and practices which lie within his field, and he must know how to find quickly the many detailed bits of information which he does not know. He must calm down the unreasonable producer who demands too much, and strive to achieve the requirements of the producer whose needs are justified. At the same time he must balance the interests of his own department with those of the service as a whole.

In so far as matters concerning the nature and content and artistic presentation of programmes are handled mainly by producers and their Heads of departments working under the Controller of Programmes, and in so far as matters of administration in a large organization are governed by many regulations, an organizer may feel that he has more responsibility than authority. He may be discouraged by the thought that almost everything that goes wrong can be attributed to a failure of organization, and little that goes right is noticeably attributable to his efforts. Although he may feel that many of his tasks are menial and concerned with details that seem to be trivial, he can be sure each day of handling matters of widely varied nature and interest. Also he knows that if his work is effective he can contribute greatly to the smooth working of a service which all the organizers believe to be well worth while.

It may be asked from where organizers come, and how they achieve the necessary qualifications? The answer cannot be specific. The organizer of each production department has a different job, requiring a predominance of different skills and different cultural interests. It may be said, however, that no young man will set out at the start of his career to become an organizer. He may drift towards it, on the tide of chance, if the various ingredients of his experience seem to add up to an appropriate whole and if his interests happen to develop in that direction. The work is largely administrative, but experience of actual programme production is a great asset.

It is thought by many that someone who has done work on programmes of the kind that is called " creative " can never attune himself to work of an administrative nature. But Michelangelo did not paint the ceiling of the Sistine Chapel in a day, and the achievements of the great composers of music depend on the mastery of technical details. The production of a television programme requires great mastery of detail in its preparation, and much work that can properly be described as administrative. The line between work which is creative and that which is not is difficult to draw.

In so far as an organizer's work amounts to the integration of many divergent factors and the reconciling of many conflicting considerations over a wide range of activities, it can provide him with great interest and also much satisfaction—particularly if he believes in the social value of the television medium.

DESIGN IN TELEVISION

RICHARD LEVIN

IT has been said that good theatre, and by that is meant the very best presentation of drama, comedy and farce, combines three essential ingredients: first-class story, first-class artistes and first-class direction. But there is a fourth ingredient that is quite as essential as the other three—the work of the designer.

In setting out the work of the designer in television and some of the problems he has to face, it is clear that a keen sense of proportion and often a sense of humour are a necessary part of his equipment to cope with all the things he is expected to do, as well as a sound knowledge of most periods in art and architecture.

Plays can be produced without scenery, and have been produced from time to time like this in television. Scenery as we know it is a comparatively modern innovation, and is part of the progress made over the centuries in presenting stage productions. Modern drama presented without scenery is an attempt to emphasize the story and artistes without any distraction or other interest. It can be quite successful, but the novelty of this method of presentation is very short-lived. It is certain that the telephone switchboard at the studios would soon be blocked if plays continued to be presented on television in this manner. Modern comedy and farce rely to a very great extent on scenery and properties to provide for the "situations" which are part and parcel of this type of show. Drama almost invariably requires realism to convince the viewer. This realism is sometimes emphasized by exaggeration to inspire even greater emotion. The use of forced perspective adds to the dramatic value of a production, together with over-sized doors, windows, etc.

Music and ballet can at times be presented without scenery. This is sometimes a matter of the subject and mood of the music and dancing, and sometimes of the personal taste of the producer. Technically, in television plain, dark or light backgrounds are not successful because on the home receiving set they give fuzz and general distortion of the picture. The ideal background is a well broken-up surface, a checker-board in fact; and, although a checker-board is obviously not a suitable backing for all subjects, the designer should have in mind that a well broken-up background is an electronic necessity and one which will give the lighting supervisor the best chance to produce a well-lit and clear picture.

The lighting supervisor has a very difficult task. Sometimes he is forgotten and then expected to provide miracles at short notice. Designing in television must therefore be a combined effort on the part of the designer and lighting supervisor. Only this collaboration will provide the clear, well-balanced pictures that viewers want to see.

In addition to sketching, researching and planning his designs, tonal colouration of the settings is an important item for the designer to take into account. Cameras used mostly for drama programmes can accept a tonal range of approximately 20 per cent. That is to say, if a strip of board is painted gradually from black at one end to white at the other, and then divided like a scale into a hundred equal divisions, any block of twenty divisions or tones can be used for set colouration without trouble from the tube in the television camera.

This happy state of affairs is not always possible to achieve, however, and an example of how critical this can be was illustrated when the lighting supervisor on a recent production asked for a cigarette to be toned down to prevent " peel off," which is an electronic distortion of the image, resulting in complete obliteration of the picture and subsequent damage to the tube if prolonged. The light catching the whiteness of the cigarette against the deep tones of the artiste's face was too much for the tube. Other cameras used for outside broadcasts and studio work have even less acceptance, but fortunately they have the advantage of needing very much less light.

The designer has to be a well-equipped man. His knowledge of any particular period of design need not be profound; in fact, if a designer is a specialist in any period, traditional or contemporary, it would be to his disadvantage as a television designer. A designer has to cope with all periods and be able to perceive the beauty and essential qualities of all ages. If a designer is a specialist he is obviously limited. Although it may be said that a specialist could produce better work than a non-specialist in a particular kind of work, it sometimes happens that a specialist becomes pedantic and fails thereby to portray the essential mood of the production. It becomes design for design's sake and not a background to emphasize and assist the action.

Often the designer's work is far removed from architectural or purely scenic design; for example, he may be required to re-produce the interior of an aircraft or space-rocket. Trains, engineering devices, the boiler-room of a ship, all require study if they are to be reproduced convincingly; at the same time the action in front of the background and the apparatus that ap-pears to work realistically and on time must also be borne in mind.

It is part of the designer's job to see that his imagination does not run away with him. He must be able to provide ideas that work; if he provides a local fog for a scene it must not disappear before the action takes place. One programme for a panel game not long ago required ping-pong balls to roll into certain slots according to the answers given by the members of the panel. It was a dismal failure; no doubt many viewers placed side bets on where the ball would appear.

Viewers sometimes wonder how solid television scenery is, whether the brickwork is really brick, or the stonework really stone. The answer generally is, no. Brickwork for television scenery is made of plaster or papier mâché, photographed on paper, or just painted, and the same applies to most of the sur-faces seen by viewers.

From time to time designers are expected to design lighter and flimsier scenery. Obviously it is to the designer's credit if he produces an effect for practically nothing, and this is frequently done. On one occasion a night scene of Paris, produced by back-projection, was not entirely successful. The designer got over the difficulty by sticking adhesive tape in a pattern to represent lights on the river front and boulevards. It went to prove that simplicity and ingenuity in design are often more successful than complicated effort and expense.

It cannot be over-emphasized that the designer's job is to

H

provide a backing completely in sympathy with the style of production. A designer can usually have freedom to experiment on a variety show, but he still has to bear in mind that tradition plays on enormous part. There are a number of things he cannot do, even in variety. He should not be stiff and formal, or observe the classic proportions of architecture too closely. Variety is generally an exaggeration of life; his backgrounds must be in tune with the mood and style of production.

Realism on the other hand is a necessity in some shows, particularly in most drama, and non-adherence can provide a crop of complaints from viewers. For example, a recent play demanded that a model train be working during part of the action. Although the play was set around 1923, the only train outfit that would operate within the area available in the scene was a "double O" gauge. Many viewers complained bitterly, pointing out that these models were not invented at that time. Mistakes avoidable and unavoidable are sometimes made, but great care is always exercised by the designers to be authentic and in period.

Since television programmes are, in the main, produced and carried out in one uninterrupted operation, much thought has to be given to planning the position of settings on the studio floor. Cameras, and there are usually three or four to a show, are connected by cables to the transmitting apparatus. It can be seen, therefore, that unless great care is given to planning on the floor, camera cables could be woven into knots. This does not happen, of course, but it could cause inconvenience and last-minute panic if the designer was not aware of the practical side of television in the studio. His sets must be placed so that the lighting on one set does not wreck the effect required on another. This again calls for close collaboration with the lighting supervisor. Sets must also be planned to enable an actor to move rapidly from one set to another when seconds and even split seconds count, particularly when an actor has to change his costume during this movement.

Room for equipment such as cameras, sound booms, dimmers, quick-change dressing booths, floor lighting, back-projection equipment, special effects, orchestras, audiences and even V.I.P.'s on occasion who want to see " how it is all done " have to be considered. Some producers like to see the set from the control-room above, as well as on their monitors in front of them. This is probably a matter of " seeing is believing " and may help some producers, but it can be extremely difficult to plan sets in a studio in this manner.

Fire regulations have to be observed. Everything used has to be fire-resisting. Some materials are taboo, such as nylon and cellulose fabrics. Obstructions to fire exits have to be avoided. Designers have to warn the fire-services that certain risks are being contemplated such as lighted torches, camp fires, candle-lit scenes, paraffin lamps, etc. Camp fires in particular are subject to close scrutiny; also explosions that may set fire to clothing and fabrics which may have lost their fire-proof qualities. Cars used in the studios during a production are allowed only one carburetter full of petrol to limit their movement. The designer has to consider room for the run-in and off again. This may be the reason why viewers have, on occasion, seen cars departing from the scene not entirely under their own power.

Materials used for building scenery are mainly wood, canvas and paint. Sometimes plaster is used, but this is heavy and cracks up very readily. Plastics are being considered to provide light ornamentation in the round. Many other materials are used to a minor degree; even screw nails exist. The search for new materials always occupies the designer.

Most materials offering a particular effect can be simulated, not always economically; but it is the designer's duty to consider the effects of materials and the possibility of simulating them, thus avoiding the sometimes considerable expense of providing the real thing. For example, beautifully panelled rooms are sometimes just paper with photographically reproduced graining and moulding; tapestries are usually provided by the scenic artists, who draw the designs with charcoal on scenic canvas; Persian carpets are painted direct on to the studio floor; balsa wood is used for furniture in fight scenes, clear toffee for glazing windows when the hero jumps right through, sawdust for sand, salt for snow and so on.

Many ideas have been put forward for building scenery by new methods : metal scenery, plastic scenery, scenery on tracks, scenery on rails, suspended and supported, revolving and folding. But the basic units for settings in most countries that have television services are still stage braces, and it would appear that this is the best method. Designers are still searching and may find quicker and better methods of providing scenery.

The designer has to provide the list of properties that are required for his production. They are divided into two categories, action properties and dressing properties. Some of the action props require a certain amount of thought; simple problems, for example, are how to make an explosion without blowing up the set, how to provide and set a fire and smoke scene without danger. Gas effects, water effects, electrical effects, all have to be planned. Recently a suite of furniture for breaking up and putting together again, both in rehearsals and transmission, was designed and made.

It would take many words to describe the numerous methods, gags and ruses the designer has to adopt to get the effects he wants. It would be true to say that one of the best qualifications a designer could have is to be able to improvise at a moment's notice. There is no time to ponder over problems. A major production is usually given only one week and sometimes less in which to be completely designed and drawn, but these limitations merely make the designer more keen to achieve the impossible.

DESIGN IN AMERICAN TELEVISION

ROBERT J. WADE

IN this brief account of scenic design in American television
it has seemed best to concentrate on the technical and economic problems that perplex and frustrate the artist in this
commercial field rather than to discuss creative approaches,
styles in design or artistic innovations.

Television, a medium of communication rather than a new
art form, is basically—so far as staging is concerned—a mixture
of theatre-films-radio.   If this is true, then any experienced stage
designer or film art director, set dresser or scenic artist should
be able immediately to take over studio art-work without the
slightest feeling of inadequacy.   In New York, especially during
the phenomenal commercial expansion of 1948-1951—when receiving sets in the United States grew from a few hundred thousand to 16,000,000—scenic men from the theatre and films designed and executed effective television backgrounds with only a
few days' actual notice and no experience except for hasty observation.   The production problems, technical, financial and
operational, were solved first by empirical means and later by
study and application.

Techniques can be learned, but control of production costs
and the devising of efficient methods of execution (preparing
scenery, costumes, properties) require considerable experience
and effort to master.   Designers learned the hard way that the
demands of commercial television are unreasonable, impossible
and unpredictable.

Unlike staging a play or musical in the theatre—a process
which now seems leisurely by comparison—producing a live
television programme involves frequent changes of script material, sometimes cancellation of entire scenes and detailed re-

planning. Because of the time element, the exigencies of studio operation (cameras, microphone booms, special effects), and because of the plurality of executives from the station, the producer's office, the advertising agency, the sponsor (and the sponsor's mother-in-law or any other connection with an opinion), the actual production, until the second it goes on the air, is kept in a state of fluidity in order to take advantage of suggestions, notes and comments provided by those who either own or control the programme.

In the theatre and films the producer and art-director work for a management that presumably is professional, that understands basically the art and craft of presentation. In commercial television the employers in the main are business men who offer a programme and buy time for its transmission in the expectation of attracting an audience of potential purchasers of the advertised product. They consequently dare not present material that might offend Methodists, say, on the one hand, or Roman Catholics on the other, or any political party or plumbers or stonemasons because individuals in these groups are buyers and users of soap, tobacco or automobiles.

All material—script or physical—is closely scrutinized and even the designer's wall decorations or set dressings are not exempt. In a recent dramatic programme I designed, I placed a crucifix on a wall behind a shot of an actress portraying an Italian-American woman praying for her son's safety. The advertising agency account executive objected. " But," I said, " I have talked with priests about the usage of symbolic objects as props and so long as they are properly employed Catholics will not be offended." " The Catholics!" retorted the agency man, " I'm worried about the Protestants."

Thus the incipient television designer, whether he is an art student or a seasoned professional in an established medium, must approach television with a very clear idea of his role in production. He must realize that, although he can maintain artistic integrity (often by indirection), he must be prepared to give and to take, to adjust and often to extemporize at the last moment when changes have to be effected. The æsthetically inclined, sensitive artist, however talented, will not be too happy in television; the more practical technical-type designer, prepared to function efficiently under less than perfect conditions, may actually enjoy the excitement of creating in shops and

118

studios, of meeting deadlines and of planning and executing designs of a qualitative level that is professional rather than academic.

The implication here is that the sponsor may not always be right or even reasonable but that, since he foots the bills, his orders must be followed. The great attention paid by advertising men to minutiæ may seem strange to the theatre-trained designer, but will not astonish the commercial artist or illustrator who is familiar with agency procedure. Petty and annoying suggestions that puzzle the designer are not the result of Philistinism, but rather develop from the advertising man's constant fear, " Will the home viewer understand what we are doing? . . . Will he turn off the set if he is bored by obscure plot convolutions? . . . Will he understand that a statue of the Venus de Milo (which the writer once thought he was using legitimately in a library set) is a work of art, and just not a statue of a naked woman?"

This attitude is not complimentary to the intelligence of thousands of viewers; but, on the other hand, ratings (percentages of viewers computed to be watching) are unfortunately the index to a programme's success, and one letter of adverse criticism may represent other complaints, percentage-wise, of persons who were too indolent to write.

These are quotations from such letters of criticism received by a New York station : " I noted the name of JOHNSON on the door of that crooked lawyer's office in your show of last night. The Johnson family, of which I am a member, objects. . . ." " I was disgusted to see that in the restaurant in the *Tomorrow* show the waiters were serving some kind of liquor. . . ." " We do not approve of our children seeing those night club scenes in your *After Dark* programme. This is an atmosphere far different from our community and one that is most un-Christian. . . ." " Your *Camera Nine* programme is usually enjoyed by us, and also some of our neighbours, but we see no point of you putting on these Russian plays like the one last night called *Cherry Orchard*, because these Communist ideas are . . ."

Designing for television, then, except for certain limitations already discussed and others of a technical nature, is little different from designing for the theatre or films. The background and training of the designer are at least the same : courses in general drawing, perspective, composition, colour, interior design, architecture, drafting and rendering, painting in still-life and landscape, history of art and as much collateral work in dramatic literature, theatre history and the humanities as time permits. It is hard to say whether a course at graduate level in the technique of scenic design or work in drawing, painting and architecture (with staging techniques to be absorbed later during an apprenticeship or by concentrated study under an established designer) is the better method of preparation.

Beyond native ability and acquired art knowledge, the designer in any presentational medium must possess a ready imagination and a sense of showmanship; he must be able to visualize details and the general effect of a locale, and subsequently be capable of realizing his concept in three dimensions. He must surmount many difficulties under pressure: producer's and director's criticism, the objections and idiosyncrasies of different groups of craft workers (who always want to do things the same way) and, in television, the perpetual race against time. Fortunately, participation in school or community dramatics provides opportunities for many potential designers to pre-judge their own capabilities before venturing seriously into the commercial field. In America, it is not unusual for student designers to work as apprentices, assistant scenic artists or stage-managers in summer stock companies to gain practical experience.

For live television, however, even the designer who already has a fine background and some basic experience needs a certain technical knowledge of the medium. The rest of this essay endeavours to convey in broad outline the essentials of this knowledge.

An electronic miracle, the camera is merely a picture-taking device so far as the designer is concerned. In production, two, three or more cameras are used to pick up action. The director pre-views each camera shot on a control-room monitor before he or a technical assistant presses a button that releases the picture for transmission. Each camera has a complement of four lenses which the cameraman changes on cue. These lenses are important to the designer because their usage determines the amount and often the quality of scenic background required. Simply stated, a 50 mm. lens on a television camera which is some 15 feet away from a setting will reveal a substantial portion of the *mise-en-scène*; a 7-inch lens at a distance of 4 feet may show only an isolated detail.

Camera " scales " for pre-planning shots are valuable, but only really practical if the designer knows precisely how the director plans to shoot a scene well in advance of rehearsals, and which lenses and distances are involved. Since live television staging is kept fluid, and since the director must work more or less by the cut-and-try method as he " blocks-out " action during his all-too-short camera rehearsals, he often cannot provide this specific information. The designer, then, usually has to furnish a larger set than may actually be required so that the cameras do not " shoot off " the edges of the background.

Much money might be saved if camera shots could be visualized (in rough " story board " sketches) and the shot established prior to scenic construction. In New York, hundreds of square feet of scenery and untold numbers of properties are wasted every week—the designer supplies them but they never show on the screen. The rapid pace of production and the limited time of " on-camera " rehearsals (a half-hour dramatic programme may have five-and-a-half hours for camera blocking and rehearsals, not including transmission time) make this wastage explainable; it is better to have too much than too little. When it is necessary to extend a setting physically because cameras are shooting off edges, the expense of labour, often on overtime, materials and transport, the matching of values or textures in painting can be exorbitant.

Frequently used camera lenses and their " picture-taking " angles are:

Focal Lengths	Approximate Angle
35 mm.	48°
50 ,,	34°
75 ,,	23°
90 ,,	19°
8-inch	8°
12 ,,	5°

These angles are constant and can be applied to any measuring scale. To make a simple camera " shot-plotter," draw any selected angle on a piece of tracing linen, bisect the angle and rule in a centre-line. This centre-line is marked off at any convenient scale (it is convenient to draw floor plans at ¼ inch to 1 foot) and represents the distance from camera lens to object or setting. This " shot-plotter " must, of course, always be applied to a plan on the same scale. The plotter indicates the widths in feet of the shot at varying distances from the camera lens. By making several different " shot-plotters " it is possible to pre-plan an entire production in advance of "dry" (without camera) rehearsals. Some directors are inclined to think that such a process, although possible, would yield a dull and static result. Most pre-plot mentally and adjust as they proceed. There is no question, however, that the plotter is very valuable to the beginning director or designer.

The picture the television system transmits is in the ratio of 3 (high) to 4 (wide). Thus small art-work, titles, miniature signs and photographs that are supposed to "fill the frame" are planned in sizes that range from 9 × 12 inches to 30 × 40 inches. In New York, a standard network size for title cards is 11 × 14 inches, with art-work centred in a 9 × 12 inches rectangle. The National Broadcasting Company's standards are: 11 × 14 inches card, 8¼ × 11 inches camera field and 7 × 9½ inches copy area.

In television settings, however, with cameras following actors, singers or dancers or panning across entire sets, it is futile for the designer to plan backgrounds in the 3:4 ratio. When the shot is very restricted and the set is planned in the aspect ratio the designer must be sure that the camera is to operate on a level and not be tilted up or down, as the results of such angulation are difficult to foresee. For example, a frequently required shot involves an actor looking out of a window into the (imaginary) street from a high office building. The designer, realizing that the scene is to be taken from a fixed position with the camera inclined upwards, builds only enough of the exterior wall of the building to border the window. He cannot know how much masking to provide at the top, so he adds more "protection" than he thinks the shot requires.

When a certain object or property is shown as an important adjunct to a scene—particularly in a commercial—the designer composes within the 3:4 ratio. In planning a small commercial set which features a refrigerator and a girl demonstrator, he can figure roughly from the height of the refrigerator and the girl (assuming she stands near the refrigerator) the probable width of the establishing shot. The width picked up by the camera is likely to be about 8 feet.

In live television, three or more cameras (one usually mounted on a 4 × 6 feet dolly carriage) and two castered microphone booms are circulating in the studio from set to set. The paths of camera movement are normally plotted by the head technician after consultation with the producer (or director) at re-

122

hearsal. In order to provide an efficient scenic layout the designer, until he becomes familiar with camera movement patterns, should discuss tentative ground plans with the technician. He may find that projected lamps, chandeliers or hanging foliage interfere with movements of the microphone boom. Changes in the preliminary plan are more economical than feverishly made alterations during final rehearsals which tie up actors, technicians, stage carpenters (an expensive lot), while some minor but perhaps noisy adjustment on the set is being made.

Both the designer and the technical camera group are dealing with difficult physical problems in a restricted working area. A great deal of tact and ability to co-operate are called for in deciding points of change or omission. If the designer has gone to the trouble of procuring a hard-to-find period chandelier for an eighteenth-century drawing-room, he may justifiably be upset at having to remove it because the microphone boom cannot swing across the set. With the producer (or director) as arbitrator, it is usually determined that the shot or means of achieving it are more important than set dressing and the chandelier is removed. But there are very likely other areas in the set where it can safely be hung. The placing of every adjunct to a scene cannot be pre-planned precisely and consequently some pictures, *objets d'art*, draperies and other dressing have to be adjusted during camera rehearsals.

The designer is responsible to the programme director (in England usually known as the producer). The director not only blocks out physical movements of actors and, broadly speaking, stages a script in an interpretative manner, but also indicates the separate shots that, with cuts or dissolves, establish the pace and mood of the programme. He is the source of the designer's information. Some directors sketch out unscaled floor plans very roughly and show by arrows or other means the principal camera angles. Others prefer to have the designer digest the script and present rough, scaled floor plans which are discussed and adjusted in conference. Sometimes, when high budgeted programmes are being planned and when time permits, the designer provides perspective sketches or even scale models. After an understanding is established between director and designer any system that works is practical.

Once the floor plan for sets is approved by the director, the designer draws a carefully scaled floor plan, indicating scenic elements, walls, doors, windows, mantels, fences, foliage, etc. From this plan he develops scaled elevations. As in other production media, construction elevations are routed to the studio carpentry department and painting details to the scenic artists.

Referring to the floor plan, the designer lists essential properties, furniture, pictures, rugs, ornaments, books, dishes (other than " hand " props), draperies, etc., which he or his assistants will procure. He also lists " greens," foliage, tree-trunks and electrical fixtures such as lamps, candlesticks, lanterns, telephones and so on.

Of course the designer cannot supervise every detail in the construction-painting-prop-gathering process; this work is the field of the Production Facilities Department which maintains carpentry, painting and property shops with drapery, titling and allied sections, as well as personnel to supervise and execute work from designs. In practice, each section charges labour and materials against the programme, plus a cost-accounting charge.

The craft services and materials needed to realize the designer's sketches are costly. The designer is governed in his spending by the requirements of the script and by the director's shot-by-shot interpretation. And because a musical, a drama or a revue programme varies weekly as to scenic locales, with collateral requirements for costumes, props, set-dressings and décors, it is difficult to work from a firm budget. I recently completed a season of sixty-five weeks as art director for *Justice*, a weekly sponsored half-hour drama. Each episode required six to eight individual sets, and these have ranged from a flooded hull of a ship, a ghostly plantation mansion and a travelling circus to modern apartments, hospital rooms and court-rooms. The weekly budget, broken down into categories and percentages of the total allocated to each section was:

	Per Cent.
Scenery (rental of units)	25
New construction	3
Properties	14
Scenic painting	12
Graphics, titling	2
Stagehands' labour	38
Make-up, wardrobe, costume design, other services	6
	100

It would appear, then, that the television designer is faced with the problem of creating both simple and complex sets for the same amount of money each week. Fortunately, within any one programme he can borrow from one category to strengthen another. The real secret, however, of operating on a small budget is in the usage, adaptation and re-usage of stock scenery and, of course, of stock furniture and properties.

The designer need not be an accountant to follow a budget, but he should apply commonsense and caution in spending. Television is expensive, and the total allotment of scenic expenses is perhaps only 14 per cent. of the entire production budget (not counting cost of air-time). As may be expected, producers do not mind stretching a point to hire stars or entertainment personalities, but do object to a penny more than budgeted for scenic investiture.

Normally, settings for television musicals and variety programmes are about the same as theatrical scenery in concept and execution. Physically, of course, they are not as high and usually do not cover a very large area (except for ballet) since they are rarely seen in their entirety. In low budgeted revues, vignette scenery is used effectively against dark blue, green or violet drapes, or sometimes against a sky cyclorama or neutral backcloth with abstract light patterns projected from above. Because scenery for variety programmes is not seen in static close-ups, it can be executed fairly crudely in a posteresque or old-fashioned scenic painting technique—it is supposed to look like scenery.

In realistic dramatic programmes, however, another situation obtains: there is an unavoidable comparison between the settings of live television dramas and that of films. The public is accustomed to realism. Theatrical canvas flats, although used a great deal in New York television, do not provide the rigidity required in realistic sets. It is difficult and labour-consuming to hang pictures, apply mouldings, architectural trim and textural treatments to framed canvas wings.

Both the Columbia Broadcasting System and National Broadcasting Company in New York have developed motion picture type "hard flats" for television in sections that can be shipped from shop to studio and be assembled and disassembled with considerable rapidity. Both networks stock hundreds of different doors, arches, windows, mantels, staircases and other units, all built in three dimensions, which fit into standard-sized openings in the basic flats. Advertising agencies or " package " producers rent these units from the networks at approximately 10 per cent. of evaluation, and pay time and materials cost, plus profit mark-up, for new construction and painting.

Conventional theatrical scenic painting, too, is employed in the fabrication of American network settings and, again, while this technique is highly satisfactory in musicals, it has only limited application in realistic sets. Because of the omnipresent costs and time problems, scenic painting (i.e., painted panels, mouldings, stencilled walls, stonework, foliage, etc.) is used to a considerable degree.

To be reasonably effective, painted work in television must be kept subdued and suggestive. Unlike the human eye, the " eye " of the television camera and its retina (the mosaic plate) cannot easily be deceived. The writer has seen painted mouldings so well high-lighted and shadowed that he has had to touch the wing to be sure they were not real; under the harsh base-lighting in the television studio, these same mouldings looked like four flat, hard lines on the system. But clever scenic artists can achieve a certain amount of verisimilitude by studying the demands of the camera.

As in films, dependence should probably be on built units and textured surfaces in realistic sets. For routine backgrounds, wing units are painted in flat tones of grey and dressed with suitable pictures, hangings, props and indicative gear. Thus, neutrally painted units theoretically can suggest a barn or an office, a living-room or an hotel lobby if they are suitably dressed. The fallacy of this kind of faking is that the designer, in saving money by using neutral flats without character, must spend more money than he normally would to rent and purchase large quantities of props to achieve the effects he wants.

Colour television is a fascinating and often beautiful medium. Although there are daily programmes telecast in colour in New York (1955), many of them of an extravaganza nature, with chorus, ballet and elaborate special effects, the adoption by the public of this new element appears to be slow. At the time of writing receiving sets for colour are about 300 per cent. more costly than standard black-and-white receivers. Production in colour is expensive, too, for the advertiser. The designer and costume designer must rent or purchase furnishings and clothes that are in acceptable colour harmony and cannot readily combine available stock items and costumes as they can for black-and-white. In black-and-white, the concentration is on value; in colour, on hue, intensity (chroma) and value.

It is impossible to present here more than a few facets of design work in television. The following check list, however, may be of value to the incipient art director. In art, rules were made to be broken, so it must be understood that these precepts are at best merely suggestive:

(1) The television screen is small; over-simplification in wall treatments, details, set-dressings and costumes is indicated. In order to show the performer effectively, backgrounds should not be " busy." Small patterns in values close to the background tone in drapes and wallpapers are better than contrasted combinations. Furniture should have simple lines and, except in Victorian interiors, dressing and details should be purposely sparse.

(2) In the main, settings should be " jogged " with recesses and reveals to provide interest and variety and to cast interesting shadows.

(3) Enlarged " photo-mural " backcloths, still and motion picture back-projection, shadowgraph effects, the use of simple types of process shots are economically adaptable to live television.

(4) The sound-stage floor is part of the picture. It can be papered or painted in suggestive textures, but the use of rugs and other coverings is impractical because of camera movement.

(5) The work of the designer is greatly simplified by a colour-response guide. Although sets may be painted in neutral tones, furniture and costumes, commercial products and dressing " come in colours " and therefore offer difficulties in value planning. In making a response guide, colours are compared to 8 or 12 different grey values on the system.

In 1952 I edited a comparative colour-response guide for the National Broadcasting Company. About 200 different hues, tints and shades were compared on camera to greys in the Munsell chart, and marked as to television grey response. Without such a guide or actual time-consuming tests it is difficult to tell whether a certain drape or costume or commercial product in, say, turquoise blue will come through darker or lighter than a background in warm tan.

(6) Wall papers are sometimes used in television sets, but generally they are too light in value or " busy " in design, and require spraying down.

(7) It should be noted that television white is 8·5 on the Munsell chart (a pearl-grey or, in colour, a light robin's egg blue). All white objects used as props are sprayed down or dipped in dye. Such items as bed linen, candles, glass curtains, newspapers, table-cloths, shirts, etc., are usually subdued with sprays or dips of light blue, light lemon yellow or light peach. The old theatrical trick of dipping too-white fabrics in coffee is frequently revived in television.

LIGHTING IN TELEVISION

ROBERT GRAY

THE main aim and purpose of a television lighting-camera-
man, or as he is more commonly called, lighting supervisor, is to provide illumination for a scene and its parts
in such a way and of such a quality as to bring out as much of
the character and significance of that scene as possible and get
it across to the viewer's set at home.

If the subject is a woman, a beautiful woman who should
look beautiful, she must be kept looking beautiful, and at the
same time her beauty must be added to by proper treatment.
Small blemishes and irregularities must be made to disappear
and her attractive features must be accented. Men, too, must
be properly handled so as to bring out their manliness, their
strength of character and so on.

Again, if the lighting supervisor is presented with a set de-
picting a fairly commonplace suburban drawing-room, with no
particular character, he may be called upon to make this room
suit the mood of a farce on a sunny day, or perhaps a bloody
murder at midnight, depending on the requirements of the
script.

One particular area of the studio may, at one moment, be set
as a garden in Spain, with hot Mediterranean sunlight for a
drama programme, and the next it is a moonlit garden café in
Vienna for a variety turn. Maybe a dentist in a science item
wants to indicate a molar with a cavity, or an archæologist show
the minute and intimate carving on a prehistoric ivory orna-
ment in a talks programme. In television, the lighting supervisor has to be qualified to meet all demands in different kinds of
programmes. A great deal of skill is required to do this consistently well.

I

Light and its companion worker shadow, properly handled, can play a large and important part in conveying the messages of television. On the other hand, badly manipulated lighting can destroy and obliterate the character of scenes and objects. Most of these problems in lighting are, in principle, of the same nature as those met with in lighting for films, still photography and, to a certain extent, the theatre.

In a television studio, however, even the simplest problem is greatly complicated by a formidable number of other factors. The greatest of these is the producer, armed with a script which can call for any number of things. Occasionally, some of these are irreconcilable in practice. In translating the script from paper to actuality, the producer creates a long list of requirements: number and size of settings, where they should be in relation to one another and the perimeter of the studio, where the cameras should be and what they should be doing when they get there and so on, through to his requirements for sound, actors, wardrobe, make-up, atmosphere and time of day in which the scene is supposed to take place.

The set designer, in putting the producer's ideas into practice, may also complicate things still further by his own views on the size, shape or colour of his settings.

The engineers demand a particular treatment of their camera apparatus so that it may function properly. Light of a certain intensity and quality must be provided to suit all the cameras, up to four in number, simultaneously, and from any angle, shooting pictures of any object within the confines of the setting—which may be interior or exterior, a day or night scene.

The dialogue from the actors or artistes must be of good quality. To do this the sound microphone-boom has to be allowed to work in any part of the setting. Nevertheless, its shadow must never appear in a picture. Through its faculty for casting shadows, the sound boom has become the lighting man's *bête noire*.

No lights can be allowed to impede the free movement of cameras, booms or actors around the set, nor must they be placed where the light may shine into the camera lenses as this would cause a ruinous flare in the picture.

There are also the varied and often conflicting demands from many other sources. The actors, the make-up artists, wardrobe mistresses, studio manager, the stage hands, the electricians and even the studio fireman have to be thought of and catered for. Over and above all this there is the very important factor of continuous action and continuous dialogue by a constantly varying cast, shot from varying camera positions. The normal solution is some form of compromise, whereby everyone is partly satisfied without departing too much from the lighting supervisor's own conception.

Having established broadly all the requirements of the production from reading the script and meeting the producer and other participants, a start is made on the lighting plot. This is marked and drawn on a reduced scale-plan of the studio to be used, which has indicated on it the outlines of the sets and the position of the cameras, etc. The various positions of the cast have been noted by attending one or more outside rehearsals some days before the programme is scheduled for transmission. To do this plotting, the lighting supervisor must bear in mind that whereas the scale-plan is two-dimensional, all lighting is three-dimensional; a mental picture of what each lamp is going to do should be formed.

There are nearly as many different techniques of lighting as there are lighting supervisors. Technique is therefore acquired individually and is highly personal, but still based on the elementary principles of photographic lighting, adapted to suit the circumstances. Large numbers of illuminators may be used on any one production, often well over one hundred lamps. They must all be used and placed effectively and accurately. At times, many of these lamps perform different functions at once, being main light, back-light or even fill-in light, depending upon which camera is in operation.

When the lighting plot is completed, it is passed to the studio electricians, who set the lamps in the positions indicated on the plot. These lamps are either hung from roof suspensions, mounted on the set itself, or placed on floor-stands. They must then be connected to their various control equipments and power supplies, still without preventing or precluding camera movement, and fitted with ancillary equipment such as diffusers, shutters, etc.

When this has all been carried out to the lighting supervisor's satisfaction, he then proceeds to put his ideas into practice by "setting" the lamps. During this operation, they are pointed in their proper directions and adjusted so that they light the correct spaces to the required brightness. The control gear is checked to make sure that the right lights can switch on or off at the proper time. Being satisfied with this, the electricians are briefed so that they can carry out their duties of switching and controlling in the correct sequence and at the right moment. The lamp setting is carried out either visually or with exposure meter, or by both methods in conjunction. All the lighting procedure, from rigging to briefing, is normally carried out in a period of about four hours. This calls for accurate and unhesitant work on the part of the supervisor.

The camera rehearsal follows. During its course, the pictures from the cameras are carefully studied. Although not physically part of his work, camera mechanics are very much the concern of the lighting supervisor, who must light for each camera set-up of anything up to four cameras which may be in movement and used in constant succession. During rehearsal maximum co-operation between the lighting man and other participants is essential to ensure the highest quality of work. Corrections to the lighting are either carried out during rehearsal or notes made to be put into effect later. There is no opportunity to reset or readjust lighting in between shots as in normal film production.

The scheduled rehearsal being completed, and as many corrections made to the lighting as possible, the programme is ready for transmission. This is the time when the lighting supervisor sees all the things he was too busy to notice during the hectic rehearsal hours!

This outline of the lighting supervisor's job is necessarily brief, many aspects having been omitted or barely mentioned, but the difficulties of the work have been accented rather than the rewards.

The job itself having been described, it is fair to ask: " What are the qualifications for this job, and how does one get to be a lighting supervisor?" In television, lighting is regarded as one of the more glamorous occupations. The lighting man is constantly in touch with the interesting, stagey side of television, meeting well-known artistes, celebrities and similar people. This sort of thing as well as his comparatively good pay makes it quite a coveted position. However, like many other jobs of this nature, it takes a lot of application and hard work to aspire to it, to say nothing of a certain amount of good luck and some ability. Lighting supervisors are made, not born, but a certain minimum of inborn capability and common sense is required.

Television lighting has, quite naturally, grown up with the medium itself. In its early days, the only people who really understood its potentialities and limitations in the technical sense were the engineers, so it was quite logical for engineers themselves to do the lighting. This state of affairs became almost traditional in the B.B.C. Television Service; it remains, for the most part, in force today. In order to be considered for a post, the potential lighting supervisor needs a solid grounding in the electronics of television engineering, mainly in the studio gear such as cameras and their associated control equipment. Hence, it is normal to enter the lighting department through the normal recruitment channels and progress through one or more engineering sections.

Over and above this background, the candidate for lighting must know something of the fundamentals of optics, light and associated subjects. He should be reasonably familiar with the functions and operation of camera equipment as well as the different types of illuminators and their fittings, including power supplies and control gear. Since sound is the lighting supervisor's biggest problem, a fair knowledge of the requirements for quality sound pick-up and recording and the means whereby this can be achieved is absolutely necessary.

Further to these, a knowledge of stage-craft, its scenery and properties, is desirable. These can greatly affect methods of work and the results obtained. Make-up and wardrobe complete the primary list of essential fields of knowledge which ought to be studied. Many of these things can be learned while still doing other jobs; most of them are learned by years of experience.

The technicalities of the job can be mastered, but they are of little use unless one learns how and when to apply them. Having learned his craft, the lighting supervisor must now master his art. The word " art " is used advisedly to mean that something which is above and beyond craft; that something which gives individuality and subtlety to one's work. In this sense the use of this word is quite legitimate. It is here, in the art of lighting, that personality and the feel for subject-matter becomes evident. Here, the first-class operator draws ahead of the average one. He can study the principles of photographic lighting and the use of light in painting, or acquire a knowledge of composition from books and galleries or even at classes, but unless he has that feel, that sensibility for the way a thing should look, then his work remains pedestrian.

As a footnote to the above, a study of the technique of good quality films is helpful. Much can be learned by intelligent observation and analysis of results and methods of top-grade lighting cameramen in motion pictures. A study also of the lighting effects of nature, in the streets, in homes and buildings, can be very instructive.

Above all, the lighting supervisor should remember that he is one of a team to serve the producer in putting on a good quality production. Television is produced at such speed, compared with film production, that diplomacy and compromise are valuable qualities in all members of the team. A ragged unit, with one technician unprepared to collaborate with another, leads always to a poor programme whose bad quality is easily discerned by the viewer and critic. Lighting is a profession, and only by striving for professional standards can quality be improved.

The above description applies to television lighting as it has been developed in Britain by the B.B.C., the only employer of lighting supervisors till recently. The possibility of employment abroad is negligible at present. This lack of an open market has tended to make the B.B.C. regarded as the sole arbiter of tastes, fashion, status and the future. This situation is in process of changing. Commercial television has arrived on the British scene, requiring experienced men for its lighting. This may extend the scope of the lighting supervisor. Already experienced staff are only numerous enough to fill a few posts; recruits must come from other places.

It is difficult to say at this date what the final developments may be, but there is already a tendency for the new programme companies to recruit this extra staff from the other branches of the advertising and entertainment industries. Still photographers may be invited, along with lighting-men from the film industry, to embark on training courses to learn the techniques of television. It appears possible, therefore, that whilst the B.B.C.'s lighting recruitment methods are likely to follow their traditional pattern, as they have at their disposal reasonable reserves of potential talent, the methods of the commercial

134

firms, of necessity, are likely to follow the other trend, and an intake of lighting staff from people already versed in the visual arts rather than in television engineering is quite possible. It is an open question as to which will prove the better way.

Regarding the number of posts available, there are at present in the B.B.C. Television Service some eighteen to twenty lighting supervisors to fulfil the needs of a single service. The advent of the commercial companies could double this figure. Future expansion when it comes will obviously increase this figure considerably, but it will be some years before the number of such posts exceeds one hundred. There is also the possibility that with the spread of television abroad, and it is spreading rapidly, overseas employment may become available to British technicians of experience.

One important subject has not been touched upon. Colour television! With its advent, the lighting supervisor could become more necessary, or conversely, he could become subsidiary to a colour consultant, or he could even be the colour consultant. That is in the future.

SOUND IN TELEVISION

R. F. A. POTTINGER

MANY television viewers are interested in producers' camera techniques and their use of visual aids. Some, indeed, become expert in recognizing who is responsible for a production before looking at the *Radio Times*, or seeing credit titles at the end of the programme. But sound is normally taken for granted. This is not surprising because television is taken to be an extension of sound broadcasting—a well-established medium—and, of course, the attention of the mind's eye is much more readily claimed than the attention of the mind's ear.

It is only when sound fails that the viewer really notices how important is the part it plays in television programmes. When this happens a most accomplished performance is reduced to an infuriatingly comic dumb show and the story is quickly lost. On the other hand, if the picture fails, the story usually can be followed fairly well for a long period by sound alone.

In many types of production the importance of both picture and sound is obvious; for example, a talk or a discussion such as *In the News*. In others, such as a dance routine in a light entertainment show, the importance of the picture is obvious, but the vital part played by sound in giving atmosphere and life is subtle.

Because viewers are so interested in visual techniques they are naturally interested in the cameramen and lighting supervisors who give the producer his picture, and correspondingly take for granted those who are responsible for the sound component of programmes. But let us now consider the men who

136

form the sound section of technicians who also work with the television producer.

For the majority of productions the sound recording team is made up of five people: the sound supervisor, two microphone boom-operators, one studio sound assistant and one gramophone operator.

The sound supervisor is responsible to the producer for all the sound aspects of a production and works near the producer in the control room. As his title implies, he is in charge of the members of his team; he decides how many microphones are to be used for a particular production, which types to use and where they are to be placed; he also operates the complicated set of knobs and switches which are arranged on the panels of the sound mixing-desk. This desk is connected via an array of amplifiers and other apparatus to the microphones in the studio, the gramophone desk, a magnetic tape machine, the sound output of a film machine, and " outside source " lines by which remote apparatus, for example an outside broadcast unit, can be connected.

In front of the sound mixing-desk there is a console containing two picture monitors and a high quality loudspeaker. One picture monitor and the loudspeaker combined give the sound supervisor his programme as the viewers will see and hear it. The other picture monitor is used to preview the picture to be transmitted from another scene, as an aid in placing microphones which are to be used later. At one side of the mixing-desk there is a gramophone desk, with four turntables and re-producing heads of pick-ups.

The two desks are installed near to the producer's desk but separated from it by a partition which contains a window. The window is normally kept down for ease of working, but can be raised by pressing a button on the sound desk so that, when the sound supervisor needs to listen very critically, he may do so without hearing the producer's directions to other people and without disturbing them by high loudspeaker volume. The sound mixing-desk is also placed near to a window overlooking the studio floor so that the sound supervisor may have a good view of the movements of artistes, cameras and microphones.

It is the job of the sound supervisor to operate the controls which fade the sources of sound into the programme as it progresses, mix them to the desired blend of sound and regulate the volume, while watching the picture on his monitor and directing the movement of the studio microphones.

The number of microphones to be used will depend on the type of production. A talk or discussion programme may require only one, but in contrast a light entertainment show will require many more. Occasionally a special production will require as many as eighteen various sources of sound, and twelve are commonly used.

A well-known example of a programme requiring only one microphone is *In the News*, in which five speakers are seated around a table. The chairman sits in the centre with two speakers on his left and two on his right. Three cameras are used: one camera takes the chairman, a second camera takes one pair of speakers and a third takes the other pair, but one microphone is sufficient because it can be suspended over the table equidistant from all five speakers and near enough to give the close sound required for close-ups of the speakers. On the other hand, typical of light entertainment productions is *Variety Parade*, which requires five stage microphones, nine for the orchestra and choir, and four for picking up applause and laughter from the audience, making a total of eighteen.

There are basically three types of microphone used for sound and television broadcasting, known as omni-directional, bi-directional and uni-directional or cardioid, according to their response to sounds. The first type responds equally well to sounds arriving from all directions. The second has two live faces opposite to each other and so responds to sounds arriving from the front and back, but not to sounds arriving from the sides or above or below. The third is sensitive to sounds arriving on one face but not to sounds from other directions, especially from behind. All three types are made in various forms and shapes and to give various degrees of quality.

Some of the very highest quality microphones must be handled with care because they are easily damaged if subjected to physical shock and may be unreliable. In the complicated process of installing settings, lights and other apparatus, such microphones are out of place for everyday use. But some of the most rugged microphones, on the other hand, do not respond faithfully to sounds and so are not good enough for broadcast quality. In between these extremes there is a choice

138

of good quality microphones which are also reliable in every-day use.

This question of reliability is very important because many television programmes have long scenes depending on one microphone and it is not an easy matter to replace one if it fails. A breakdown through faulty vision is serious enough, but under-standable in view of the complexity of the electronic apparatus involved; sound equipment is simple and straightforward by comparison and should not fail.

Fortunately it happens that the very finest quality of sound reproduction is most appreciated in music items. For these it is often possible to use the very best microphones and safe-guard against breakdown by using two with one as standby. Most everyday transmissions involving speech do not permit this, but the fine difference between good and very good repro-duction of speech is unimportant to the ear.

To meet all these conditions, television studios are equipped with a range of microphones which are used according to the circumstances of each production.

Another reason for having a range of types of microphone is the need for directional microphones in television. Many pro-ductions, especially plays, have the actors arranged in small groups for several scenes. An omni-directional microphone, capable of picking-up sound from all directions as its name indicates, is very suitable for this purpose. Unfortunately, in the normal course of events there are other things being done which can be heard by such a microphone: cameras moving to their positions for the next scene, parts of scenery being shifted, actors moving into position, and so on. All these movements are necessary but they contribute to annoying off-stage noise, and to reduce this noise cardioid microphones are commonly used. This is the type which is most sensitive to sounds arriv-ing on one face; since most of the unwanted noises occur on the side of the microphone opposite to the artistes the microphone can be turned towards the artistes and away from the inter-fering noise.

Most television productions involve frequent changes of scene and also actors must be free to move about within each scene. Indeed, a great deal of interest and excitement can be created by a proper control of movement, and all technical equipment, including microphones, must be free to follow actors' movements. The equipment must, also, be quickly moved from one scene to another.

One important difference between camera and microphone is that the camera can take a close-up picture without actually being close to the scene if a telephoto or narrow-angle lens is used, whereas the microphone must be kept fairly near to the artistes all the time. If the microphone is too distant, even if the picture is of a distant scene, the sound loses clarity and becomes indistinct. This means that, as the actors in a play move about, the microphone must follow them to pick up their voices. To make this possible the microphone is mounted at the end of a long telescopic arm, known as a boom. The weight of the microphone is balanced by a set of weights at the opposite end of the boom arm, and this balanced assembly is mounted on a pivot so that the microphone can be moved through a wide horizontal or vertical arc, or both together.

The microphone boom has a cradle at the microphone end so that the cardioid microphone can be turned and tilted by cords joined to controls farther along the boom arm. The boom is mounted on a wheeled base and fitted with a platform upon which the microphone boom operator stands; this operator is able to extend and retract the telescopic arm, elevate and swing the arm, and twist and tilt the microphone in its cradle, all by two hand controls.

The tricky work of handling this piece of equipment requires the degree of mental co-ordination employed to pat one's head with one hand, while at the same time rubbing the chest with the other!

The microphone boom-operator is primarily concerned with keeping his microphone in a suitable position to pick up the sounds made by the artistes being televised, according to their movements in the scene and according to the position of the camera. If the camera tracks into a long-shot the microphone must be moved away and up a little to give the aural effect of distance, and if the camera tracks into a close-up the microphone must be moved closer accordingly. At the same time, the microphone must not be allowed to dip into the picture, nor must it cast a shadow on the artistes' faces or the scenery. This procedure is made very complicated in most television productions by the use of more than one camera, often four, in any one scene; and each camera has four lenses, enabling the producer to vary the size of shot from close-up to long-shot without movement of the camera itself.

It is usual to have two microphone booms in a television production, each with its own operator. Sometimes both are used in one sequence to cover movement over wide acting areas and to cover dialogue between two characters who are being taken in close-up but at opposite sides of the set. In such a case each actor will be seen by his own camera and heard by his own microphone. At the end of a scene, or towards the end, one boom must be available in the next scene in another part of the studio. If the action allows one boom will be moved at a prearranged time, but if the action does not permit this a third boom must be in position in readiness. The third boom will be operated by the sound floor-assistant who is the junior of the trio working in the studio; this man also " tracks " the other two booms and their operators when action takes place out of normal reach, and is responsible for any other microphones and sound equipment, such as the microphones mounted on floor stands.

The senior man of this studio trio operates the microphone boom which takes the bulk of work or the most difficult work. In addition he is deputy to the sound supervisor and takes over sound mixing in small productions to allow the supervisor to go to planning meetings or outside rehearsals for a future production; he also replaces the supervisor if he is ill or on holiday.

It is clear that this team of operators must be able to work together with considerable understanding of each other's difficulties, to co-ordinate the positioning of microphones with movements of artistes and cameras.

The gramophone operator works in the control-room with the sound supervisor. His job is to play gramophone records of introductory music, incidental music and special recordings of sound effects noises.

Many gramophone operators are also expert microphone boom operators, so that, after suitable experience in these jobs and if they have the operational ability and personal qualities of judgment, they may graduate through the position of relief sound supervisor to take charge of the sound team as sound supervisor.

SPECIAL EFFECTS IN TELEVISION

D. R. CAMPBELL

A T the turn of the century, early pioneers in the film industry became fascinated by the trick effects and optical
illusions obtainable by the movie-camera itself and by
manipulation of the subjects photographed by it. The trick
films of Georges Méliès, the Frenchman, have become classic
primitives of the art of the cinema. In fifty-odd years, almost
every major film studio has set up its own special effects department to handle problems which may call for the use of
small-scale models (miniatures), trick mirror effects, optical devices carried out in the laboratory and amazing illusionary processes such as the travelling matte.

The special effects man is recognized as a highly skilled technician with resources of imagination, artistic good taste and an
experience of the technique of motion pictures. Broadly speaking, his task is to create an effect on the cinema screen not possible by normal methods of studio or exterior filming.

Still in its infancy, television is already developing its own
processes of special effects, and these are likely to offer increasing scope for the technician with an urge to experiment and to
utilize his powers of ingenuity.

What does the term special effects conjure up in our minds?
Do we mean a magical scene of, say, a flying-carpet, a headless
dancer, or do we infer an illusion of a realistic scene such as a
ship in a storm or a railway smash? All scenes of the former
type, which the viewer knows must be some form of trick, are
best described as magical; while the latter are realistic, that is
to say, the viewer should be able to accept them as the real
thing. The scene of a ship at sea in a storm or the flashing past

of a landscape through the windows of a railway train, while realistic in character, are termed special effects because their production calls for special apparatus operated by specialized staff.

There are also shots which are neither magical nor realistic, being a particular way of presenting the action or story. For example, there are various forms of split-screen working. In a reality programme, one half of the picture can be a scene in Birmingham and the other half a scene in London. In a studio production the script may call for a reporter to be ringing up his news-editor from the scene of the crime; this picture on the screen might be divided into two areas so as to knit the two scenes together although taking place at locations miles apart.

The television script-writer is apt to regard the technique of his medium as technically limitless and to think that any scene or situation he may like to devise is possible, especially if the effect he requires is commonplace in the film industry. The difference in the time factor of making a film and producing a television programme is often forgotten. It is probable that technically, time being available, television is able to produce all the trick effects used by the film industry.

In practice, however, trick shots in British television have been kept to a minimum because of the time taken to arrange them. A special effects shot may last only thirty seconds in an hour's television production, but it may require sixty minutes or more of valuable rehearsal time to prepare. There is, therefore, a tendency at the present stage of production to keep such trick work to an absolute minimum in telling a story. Many shots which a writer or producer have in mind, coming under the heading of " trick," have to be eliminated at early planning stages because of this time factor.

In spite of the time problem, however, special effects are used in television and their use is increasing. Technically, some of the methods are common to both television and film—and even to the stage. The first special effect used in television was the superimposition; that is to say, the electrical mixing of two or more pictures to produce either the conventional form of a ghost shot or certain types of montage.

The ghost effect achieved by superimposition is relatively simple to produce; one television camera shoots the general scene while the other takes the ghost played in front of a plain, dark background. As all conventional ghosts are in a high key after superimposition, only the ghost appears in the required scene or final picture, the plain, dark background not being reproduced. Technically, ghosts formed by this easy method have improved as the performance of television camera tubes has progressed. To achieve the superimposition effect technically requires only the turn of two or more knobs, the intensity of any given picture being controlled by the number of degrees turned. Ghosts have also been produced by optical means, using the well-known Pepper's ghost effect.

While superimposition of one visual image over another may be used for montage effects, it is often necessary to inject part of one picture into part of another without superimposition or ghost effect. This is done by what is known as vignetting. It is a process by which one area of a picture is gradually shaded into another, a method used to shade off the background of a photographic portrait into white or black.

In television production vignetting is always used in conjunction with superimposition. It is achieved by placing a suitable mask between the camera lens and the scene, about two focal-lengths distance in front of the lens. The mask is generally made of cardboard so shaped as to allow the lens to see the wanted part of the scene but at the same time blocking out the unwanted. The line of demarcation between the wanted and unwanted areas fades into each area more or less indefinitely according to the distance of the mask from the lens. The nearer the mask to the lens the more diffused the result, the tone value of the unwanted area being a function of the tonal value of the mask on the side next to the lens. In television this is nearly always black. Two cameras are used for the required effect.

For example, suppose for some script reason a different scene is required in each diagonal half of the screen. One camera would have a diagonal mask placed in front of its lens so that only a portion of the scene before it is reproduced, while the other camera would have the same sort of mask but in the opposite sense. In both cases the mask would vignette the unwanted half of its picture into blackness. The pictures so obtained by the two cameras would then be electrically superimposed (or mixed) and the required result would be achieved—that is to say, a composite picture of two completely different scenes gently fading into each other, the hardness of the line

144

dividing the two scenes being adjusted, as already described, to suit the requirements of the production. Small areas in one picture format can be selectively vignetted in the same way, such as a live scene into the frame of a picture. It is necessary in nearly every case for the two vignetting masks to be fixed one to each camera.

The special effects of vignetting have been used extensively, even to the point of vignetting scenes from a film into the live scenes in a studio. Similarly, the use of much scenery has been saved by judiciously vignetting a small but full-scale studio scene into a portion of a still photograph. For example, a drama production called for a scene of a dictator haranguing a crowd from a castle parapet. This was economically done by selecting a suitable still photograph and vignetting in a small set, full-size, of the battlements with the actor in live action. The studio set had, of course, to be carefully constructed to fit into the photograph. The camera shot was decided in detail at the planning stage, for the relatively short rehearsal time in the studio cannot be taken up too long over one shot.

One of the problems of using vignettes is that two cameras must have special fittings to carry the masks. These fittings take time to position, which means that two of the usual four cameras used in a studio production are out of action for a certain time before the shot in question is required. It thus became obvious that if some form of vignetting could be invented which eliminated any fittings on a camera, it would be an advantage. This requirement is now satisfied to a large extent by the use of what is known as Inlay. It is a form of electro-optical device by which one common mask controls the signal from both cameras. The system, however, suffers from the disadvantage that it gives a very defined dividing-line between one picture area and another. This æsthetic drawback is to some extent offset by the fact that more effects can be obtained during one production without waste of cameras.

The broad principle of the Inlay apparatus is an electronic switch which is controlled by the amount of light falling on the photocell, the light being produced from an unmodulated cathode-ray tube whose scanning is synchronized with that of the cameras. Masks cut from opaque material are placed on the special cathode-ray tube. Where the mask is opaque it prevents the light from the raster from reaching a photocell, which in turn operates the electronic switch in favour of one camera; where the mask is non-existent the light reaches the photocell and the second camera is favoured. To split the picture in two so as to have a different scene on either side, it is necessary only to cover up half of the raster of the special cathode-ray tube with a piece of card. The two cameras producing the final picture can be any distance apart.

As already stated, Inlay can produce a more extensive range of effects than camera vignetting. For example, the drawing of an opaque mask across the light-producing raster will obviously gradually obliterate the light from the tube and the effect seen by the viewer is a "wipe" from one scene to another. It is possible to fade or cut in-and-out one portion of the picture without affecting the other. Another effect is to write across a scene so that the viewer actually sees the letters being formed; or the converse can be done, that is to say, wipe a title either quickly or slowly in or out of a scene.

The following are some examples of what has been done by Inlay. In a certain programme there was a scene of two men (one a magician) looking into a mirror in which there was a reflection of themselves. As they looked, the scene in the mirror dissolved to that of a man and a woman. A somewhat similar effect was that of an actor looking into a mirror, seeing himself, and then his reflection dissolving into somebody else. In a somewhat complicated production a magician set up his box to saw a woman in half and one half of the woman ran out of the box, followed later by the second half chasing her first. Many of the common effects, such as the view of the passing landscape through a carriage window, are produced by this apparatus.

In a programme series the opening scene of each production called for a picture of the *corps de ballet* rehearsing on the stage of an empty theatre seen from the back of the stalls. To produce the effect, the stage of a well-known theatre was photographed from the required position and the dancers in the studio Inlayed into the photograph, the studio floor replacing the stage, thus saving a very large and costly set.

The same principle is used to produce an animated Christmas card, or again the Inlaying of a sea scene from a ship. In this case, of course, the Inlayed effect is a mixture of a studio scene and a film. The split-screen effect of a commentator in a

146

London studio talking to an interviewee in, say, Birmingham is brought about by the Inlay process. In this last example, Genlock has to be used as well—that is, electronic apparatus which brings London into synchronization with distant Birmingham which are normally in isochronism.

Closely associated with Inlay is a process known as Overlay. This is a method for putting the foreground of one scene in front of the background of another. The working principles are as follows.

The foreground scene is arranged in front of a plain black or white background. The lighting is so controlled that in the case of the black background none of the foreground is darker than twice the brightness of the background (or with the white background, the foreground must not be brighter than half the brightness of the white background). A two-to-one brightness difference is required in both cases. To achieve this, apart from careful lighting, the reflectance values of the foreground have to be selected; for example, no black on a dress in the case of a black background and vice versa. The resultant signal of the foreground scene is electronically conditioned and then applied to the signal of the background scene (which may be a studio, an outside broadcast or a film scene) in such a way as to produce a " hole " or black silhouette of the foreground scene, after which the normal tonal values of the foreground are electronically fitted into the " hole " or silhouette. The result is a foreground scene put in front of a different background scene.

The Overlay process at present is not wholly satisfactory for a realistic effect, but for magical illusions it can be most successful. While Overlay normally requires two camera sources of picture, with a third camera one can fill the silhouette of the foreground with another picture.

A magical use of Overlay is, for example, to reduce a human being to the size of a doll: a doll dances in a children's toyshop while full-sized children look on in amazement. The alteration in size called for by a production such as *David and Goliath* is another instance. In this particular programme Goliath was a normally tall man, but David was reduced in size by taking a relatively long shot of him and Overlaying it into the Goliath scene, thereby solving the casting problem of finding a man twelve cubits high.

Another magical effect depending on Overlay was a scene of

147

a conjuror who tears some paper and produces a row of little men. He then bundles up the paper and throws it down in front of him. Out of it comes one little paper man who climbs up and sits on the conjuror's shoulder, does a few antics and eventually retires to vanish into the paper from where he started. This was done by the use of three cameras and Overlay. Camera One represented the background, which in this case was the conjuror and his paraphernalia. Camera Two acted as the Overlayed foreground, which was a puppet in front of a plain white background. Electrically the image of the puppet produced a silhouette in the background scene, the space being filled in not by the image of the puppet itself but by a picture of a piece of newspaper. During this particular special effect the puppet operator had to control the strings by watching the result of the composite picture on the television monitor screen and working accordingly.

On the realistic side a sports commentator in the London studio was made, by Overlay, to appear to be sitting on a bench beside a greyhound owner in Newbury. While holding an interview, the commentator was apparently patting the man's greyhound, which was actually many miles away.

Back-projection both of still and moving pictures has been used in television for some years. The background settings for some plays have been wholly dependent on back-projection, using four screens and two projectors so arranged that by the aid of mirrors one projector can throw its slide on to one of the two screens. This process unfortunately requires a considerable amount of floor-space for the throw of the projector, but in practice the throw is always folded back on itself by use of a mirror. The slides or plates are always photographic, generally of an actual scene. There are productions which require a more stagey setting, and on these occasions photographs are taken of drawings.

One of the advantages of back-projection is that, when a large number of backcloths is required, there is a great saving of time in setting scenery. Lighting of the various cloths is also reduced, one lamp and one rigging process producing an infinite number of scenes. Back-projection requires rather more care in lighting the studio set in general since any stray light falling on the screen must be kept to a minimum.

Technical apparatus used for the back-projection of still

148

photographs is best described as a very high-powered magic-lantern whose light source is an arc capable of burning up to 220 amps. Elaborate precautions are taken to filter out the heat component of the light by passing it through a water-bath to absorb the heat, while the slide is cooled by a special compressed-air system. Considerable use is also made of small projectors of the filmstrip type. These are used on the back-projection principle, the picture being projected to about 12 × 15 inches, the material being specially prepared slides, such as illustrations from books or paintings in art galleries.

In the case of the back-projection of moving pictures a standard form of film projector is used with, however, a special shutter arrangement. Here a main technical difficulty is the fact that a film projector requires a relatively long time to move the film from one picture or frame to the next, relative that is to the time between individual pictures of the television system.

The preparation of the slide or film for back-projection calls for careful planning, especially as to viewpoint and size of image if correct or acceptable perspective is to be maintained. Further, the lighting of original scenes from which the slide is prepared must be in keeping with that of the studio set with which it has to be married. A high standard of photographic quality is necessary throughout. Moving back-projection, apart from its technical problems, is expensive if used for any length of time, which mitigates against its use.

Closely allied with back-projection is the use of relatively small cut-outs whose shadows are arranged to fall on a back-projection screen. The size and form of shadow is a matter of the position of the light sources used to produce the shadows. Shadows from moving cut-outs and lights can produce a most figurative effect.

Occasionally, for a magical trick, use is made of coloured lights or coloured filters. If a human face is given a specially selected green make-up and is televised when lit by green light or through a green filter, the actor can be made to appear as a white-skinned person. By changing the light or the filter from green to red, a dark-skinned effect is produced. The same method has been used on certain diagrams, such as maps, where it has been desired to show a given outline and then emphasize a particular area. In such a case the diagram, which is to be visible all the time, is drawn in black-and-white while the area

149

that is to be made to stand out is drawn in red. If lit by a similar red light this latter area is invisible, but by changing the filter to green the required area gradually builds up to an intense black.

The same process was used in a drama production to produce the effect on the television screen of a man being burnt at the stake. In the studio the victim was tied to a pyre of faggots. Superimposed on to this picture was a bonfire (previously filmed). The changing of the coloured lights plus the make-up referred to above produced a realistic and frightening effect of the burning of the Wandering Jew.

Many special effects are produced by the property and art department. Their products vary from a conjuror's properties to scale models; from animated drawings to practical fog and smoke. Models appear to be employed less than in the past for direct television. Little recourse has been had to the animated scale models used in the film industry. The problem of reducing the speed of movement in the model (to match its scale) is more difficult to achieve in television since no variation of taking speed is possible as is the case with films.

The shot taken through a painted-glass foreground, used in the film industry, is occasionally employed, but in television this is more easily done by Inlay, though in both cases the time factor reduces their use. One of the major problems in a lot of television trick work is the difficulty of keeping the size of the images constant owing to slight variations of electronic scanning on which all television picture sources are dependent.

Mirrors in various forms also play their part. Unusual reverse shots are taken through half-silvered mirrors where the camera must not be seen. The old-fashioned kaleidoscope has been revived in television to give special presentation of photographs and drawings.

Turning to the future, it is safe to say that special effects in the widest sense are only in their infancy, and it is certain that any television service will require a specialized staff to run this department. It is interesting to consider what type of individuals will be required. Probably they will be divided into two main categories—those who make the television system see things differently from the way the eye sees and those who make the " specials " which the eye normally perceives. The former must know the optical-electronic aspects of television in all its ramifications and obviously must come from the ranks of television technicians or engineers, while the latter will include the model-maker, the " gadget genius " and the art designer. Both must have imagination, the visual sense of what is a good picture, the power of getting into the producer's mind by understanding his requirements and, last but not least, the sense of showmanship that the show must go on.

THE SCOPE OF TELEVISION

WILL TV LINK THE WORLD?

HENRY R. CASSIRER

TELEVISION is becoming a world phenomenon. First developed in the industrially most advanced nations—principally in France, Germany, Japan, the Netherlands, the Soviet Union, the United Kingdom and the United States—television has long since spread beyond its original industrial base. Not only have telecasting stations been set up in most industrial nations of Europe and North America, but there are today television systems in many countries without a trace of an electronic industry, from Cuba to Venezuela, from Morocco to the Philippines.

At the beginning of 1955 television stations broadcast regularly or on an experimental basis in thirty-eight countries or non self-governing territories, and another twenty countries in every continent were seriously studying its introduction. Not a month passes without reports of additional countries who are taking steps to introduce a television system. Television has become a significant attribute of the modern state. Within a few years there will hardly be an important country without it.

This powerful new medium of mass communication has, however, reached true mass proportions in only a few countries. Three countries—the United States, the United Kingdom and Canada—have more than a million receivers, while a fourth, the Soviet Union, is approaching this mark. Elsewhere the number of receivers rarely exceeds 200,000. In many countries sets can be counted only by thousands. Television is still in its formative stage. Any predictions about its future shape must therefore be made with great caution. Thanks to its uncanny audience attraction, to the growth of collective reception supplementing viewing in the family home, and thanks to technological advances which are liable to reduce considerably the price of receivers, it may, however, be foreseen that within a relatively short time television will have dominant mass influence in many nations. What does this portend for communication between them?

The speed and extent of international development will depend fundamentally upon technical progress. While black-and-white television in all countries is based on the same technical principles, the standards adopted for telecasting vary considerably. There are at present five major "definitions" in use, plus a number of minor variations. That means that television programmes cannot automatically cross from one area to the other. It is as if railway systems in neighbouring regions were using a number of different gauges and trains had to be adapted every time they crossed the border.

Fortunately, two developments are helping to overcome this obstacle to international communication by television: pictures can be converted optically from one definition to the other, and sets are being constructed for sale in border regions which can receive more than one definition. Both means have, however, their drawbacks. Conversion not only requires additional expensive installations but makes a certain loss of quality inevitable, while multiple definition sets are more expensive than ordinary sets. Yet the growth of Eurovision, which includes three major definitions (819 lines in France, 625 lines in Central Europe and 405 lines in the United Kingdom, as well as variations of these definitions in Belgium), has demonstrated that definition frontiers can be successfully overcome.

The only way in which programmes can be sent from country to country irrespective of the definition problem is by way of film. The increasing availability for telecasting of film made by the motion picture industry for showing in cinemas, the rapid growth of film production specifically for television use and the telerecording of programmes furnish ample material for international exchange. Film has the drawback that it eliminates one of the most fascinating aspects of television, the instantaneous transmission of picture and sound. Yet it has many advantages over live transmissions. It is not subject to limitations with regard to time and place of broadcast. Telecasts on film can be preserved, repeated and shipped anywhere in the world. Their manner and time of transmission can be adapted more easily to foreign audiences. And the cost of re-broadcast via film is minimal compared with the cost of constructing and maintaining permanent relay links. Moreover, films, other than telerecordings, do not produce any loss of quality from one country to the other.

A third technique which may also be important for international television communication is the recording of the television signal on magnetic tape. While still in its experimental stage, it promises to reach perfection within a relatively short time. It will then be possible to record and reproduce live telecasts without any loss of quality. Yet here, too, there will be a time lag between origination and re-telecast, and it remains to be studied whether magnetic tape can be reproduced on a television system with a different definition without complicated conversion.

The technical problems are only one aspect of the issues which must be faced in efforts to send television programmes across national borders. How can a programme be made acceptable to an audience with a different cultural and linguistic background?

While the picture, with its universal appeal, is the heart of television, the word remains its essential complement. In major countries of Europe where there is no widespread knowledge of foreign languages, the popular audience appears to resent strongly television programmes in which a foreign language is spoken. Even if the foreign words are later translated, the audience reacts with a mixed inferiority-superiority complex (" I wish I could understand what they are saying "—" Why can't they speak our own language?"). And every translation is bound to slow down the pace of the telecast. Nevertheless, the presence of bi-lingual commentators in telecasts must not be excluded as a possible technique, for television offers the advantage, compared with the radio, that even if the viewer does not understand the words he has always something to see. In 1952 the B.B.C. and French Television telecast a visit to the Louvre in Paris in which a British and a French commentator alternatively explained its sculpture collection. This telecast had a fair appeal in Britain because viewers could admire close-ups of Michelangelo's sculptures while the French commentator described them to his own audience.

How else can language differences be overcome? Here experience of the cinema is unfortunately of little help. Sub-titles are practically useless on television because they are cut off or unreadable on most home receivers, unless they are placed so high on the screen that they obscure the scene. Moreover, whenever an event is telecast instantaneously there obviously is no time to make sub-titles. Nor is it feasible under these conditions to use the other method employed by the cinema, dubbing. Dubbing remains a useful if expensive technique for making foreign versions of films produced for television. This is confirmed by the recent experience of American producers who are releasing their product to French, German, Italian and Spanish markets.

The method currently employed in the direct relay of live telecasts within Eurovision is to depend entirely on off-screen commentaries in the national language. Generally national commentators are sent to the scene of the event and make their narration on the spot. If that is for some reason not possible, an alternative and much less satisfactory method is for the commentator to narrate from the screen in his home country while listening to a " guide line " from the country of origin.

Off-screen commentary appears also the most feasible and economical way for the adaptation of films and filmed programmes, provided these do not contain any important lip-synch. dialogue sequences. That is why television stations are now beginning to produce their filmed programmes with an international music and effects sound track. This sound track can be sent to another country together with a written script which is telecast there in a different language. Such commentaries can also cover shorter lip-synch. dialogue sequences, e.g., interviews with important personalities. But dramatic programmes can obviously not be reproduced adequately by this technique. In this connection the experience of Russian television which telecast the performances of the Comédie Française in Moscow is particularly interesting. Here the commentators confined themselves to summarizing the action before and after each act of the play and audiences frequently followed the programmes with the French text or its translation in hand.

There remain two important techniques which avoid the language problem altogether.

One is to make foreigners who participate in the telecast talk your own language. When American television produces dramatized detective stories in Europe it may import certain lead actors, but most performers are recruited from English-speaking Europeans. And when B.B.C. reporters go to India or Germany they can interview a sufficient number of English-speaking foreigners so that the home audience will not have to hear any foreign tongue at all. This technique can of course be employed only in broadcasts destined for one particular language audience.

The other method is to select programmes which require no commentary whatsoever. French television puts on hour-long variety shows, even for its own audience, which consists merely of a well-staged series of acts, with the names of performers briefly shown to the viewer in superimposition.

With the language problem out of the way, we arrive at the most difficult of all issues: the content of programmes suitable for reception by many nations. Experience here is still extremely limited, and theories may easily be propounded without fear of being proven wrong. Within the limitations of this essay it is not possible to enter into the psychological and æsthetic subtleties involved. A few general remarks will have to suffice.

In international live television the lead is undoubtedly taken by events of major international importance and appeal, and by sports contests of international significance. The two most successful relays have been the Coronation of Queen Elizabeth of England and the world football cup matches in Switzerland, which were the corner-stone of the birth of Eurovision. But how many events of this kind take place week after week? There follows then a whole series of programme types, each offering their particular attraction and their special problems, such as folk festivals and variety shows, portraits of the lives of ordinary people or of famous men, visits to national shrines and reports from places of particular artistic, scenic, social or economic significance.

In all of these and other telecasts two questions always plague the producer: if the programme is of international as well as of national interest, should it be presented primarily with the foreign or with the domestic audience in view? And is it worth while to utilize the expensive international relay network for a live telecast with its necessary limitations in scope and time, or would a film be a more suitable means for portraying the scene and conveying it to foreign audiences?

Live programmes are the champions of international television. But films maintain their importance. Films can treat subjects more flexibly, they can be carefully adapted to foreign languages and they can be organically integrated into national programming. The greatest problem in all telecasts from abroad is how to make the link between the foreign scene and the preoccupations of the home audience. To cite a specific instance, a British, American or German commentator visiting a foreign country and recording his impressions on film, provides the necessary identification for the home audience so that the viewer feels he has been on the tour. A national commentator integrating a foreign film into his programme, whether it be a children's show or a newscast, a telecast on art or on travel, will more easily build this necessary bridge. For all experience indicates that programmes require skilful adaptation to make them acceptable to a foreign audience.

Is it only the strange, the exciting, the spectacular which appeal to audiences in telecasts from abroad? The evidence indicates that this is by no means so. People like to see how other people live, they wish to have an intimate view of the life of man and the face of nature in places to which they cannot hope to go themselves. Audiences welcome enrichment of their cultural life through the creative arts of other nations and other civilizations. The form and content, the new style of international programmes will thus be determined by the needs of the medium, the material suitable for telecast and the desires of the many audiences.

There remains a further group of problems to be solved in the production of programmes for international consumption: the whole gamut of issues linked to copyright and performers' rights. The creative or performing artiste, the producer and distributor, represented by their professional associations, television and film organizations, they all claim their share and benefit in this world-wide programme distribution. Present legal and technical machinery is ill-adapted to these new developments. It will take years of fumbling practice, of *ad hoc* solutions, of patient, equitable negotiation, as well as the creation of new machinery and new types of contracts to pave the way for a free flow across national borders of every kind of television programme.

The live exchange of television programmes made its spectacular beginning in Europe during the months of June/July, 1954, when eight countries (Belgium, Denmark, France, Germany, Italy, the Netherlands, Switzerland and the United Kingdom) relayed the world cup football matches from Switzerland and each contributed at least one programme for re-telecast by the rest. This experiment of crowding relays into a limited period was repeated during the Christmas season of that year. Nineteen fifty-five has seen a change in the pattern. The success of the first experiment is stimulating the construction of permanent relay links, and telecasts are now transmitted when the event warrants it rather than scheduled arbitrarily during a limited period. Moreover, programmes are not always carried by all Western European television countries. Bi-lateral or tri-lateral exchanges frequently make it easier to overcome the technical, linguistic and content problems involved.

Regular live transmissions also take place between the United States and Canada, where they are favoured by geographic proximity and the fact that most of Canada's television stations transmit in English. Television programmes for the first time crossed the ocean when Cuba telecast the World Series baseball games in September, 1954. Stratovision, re-transmission of the television signal by an aeroplane circling halfway between the stations in Florida and Cuba, was used to bridge a distance too wide to permit direct pick-up.

Outside of these two areas, and even within them, programme exchange and international distribution is being developed by means of film. Throughout Latin America stations transmit television films made in the United States. Similarly American producers are offering their films to stations in Europe and Japan. The B.B.C. carries telerecordings of American programmes, such as Edward R. Murrow's *Person to Person* and *See it Now*. Inversely, the B.B.C. is promoting transmission of its own programmes on American and Canadian television, while Latin American stations are examining the exchange of filmed or telerecorded programmes among each other.

Film originally not made for television, including feature films, Westerns, travelogues, documentaries and cartoons, form a large proportion of the programmes of most television stations. Much of this film is imported from abroad, and international film distribution is making rapid strides.

L

A third form of international programme co-operation is the adaptation of programme formats and the exchange of producers. Quiz, discussion and variety programmes all have their peculiar forms in which they can most effectively be carried on television. Stations lean on each other's experience in adapting them to their own needs. Well-known British examples are *Animal, Vegetable, Mineral?* as well as *What's My Line?*, both British adaptations of American examples. This exchange of experience is further helped through an exchange of producers. The B.B.C. has telecast science programmes with American producer Lynn Poole, and dramatic or variety shows with French producers Claude Barma and Margaritis. In turn British producers Andrew Miller-Jones and Alvin Rakoff have gone to America and France to stage their own version of television programmes on these foreign stations.

The beginnings of 1955 are mere indications of what the future holds. Development of a relay network in Eastern Europe paralleling Eurovision in the West is under active study, and responsible officials of Western television already speak of future links from London to Moscow and from Stockholm to Sicily. To join North American television with this European network a transatlantic relay from Canada through Greenland, Iceland and the Faroe Islands is being seriously examined. Despite its great expense (estimated at $50 million), despite the technical problems involved and the time differential with its effect upon the scheduling of telecasts, responsible representatives of industry and government envisage such a link within the next decade.

Yet it would be unrealistic to believe that these direct relays will become the dominant form of international programme co-operation in the near future. Film will maintain and enlarge its prominent place. New types of film programmes will make their appearance. Instead of producing for a national market and then seeking adaptation and distribution to foreign stations, producers will begin to create programmes from the start for international distribution. International television will become a market in its own right. And television stations, together with national film production centres, will create programmes by pooling their resources, by co-producing shows in which each nation makes its significant contribution. The scope of the final programme thus exceeds anything a national organization would have been able to create out of its relatively limited resources.

The first conference on the international co-operation of film and television, held at Tangier in September 1955 under the auspices of Unesco, demonstrated the desire to promote programme exchange by film as well as the many obstacles which will have to be overcome. The meeting envisaged the creation of an International Centre of Films for Television. Such a Centre might contribute to the normal workings of international film distribution, to bilateral sales and exchange agreements and to the growth of live relay networks in aiding television to become the show window of the world.

What will be the significance of this new venture? What are its importance, its dangers and its opportunities?

Television is already the most centralized of all media of mass communication. Its programmes are determined by the smallest number of men who are operating from the least number of production centres and exercising a maximum control over the viewing public, to whom they are offering a minimum of choice.

The printed word can be written by everyone and published by a great number, so the reader has choice among many publications. Film production is more centralized. But there is no technological obstacle to the formation of new production units while the audience is offered multiple alternatives among national and foreign films. Radio, utilizing the public broadcast frequency, has made an important step toward centralization. Nevertheless, the relatively limited cost of radio production makes it easier to duplicate broadcast services, and the audience can tune in to numerous national as well as foreign programmes.

But television is restricted both on the producing and the receiving end. Like radio it is subject to government regulation as it uses one of a limited number of telecast frequencies. Yet unlike radio it requires very great capital resources for the installation and operation of a station. And again unlike radio the transmissions of a television station only reach a limited area so that viewers can choose at best among a small number of programmes.

Television everywhere has difficulty in giving adequate expression to regionalism and serving the multiple preferences of the public. This is true even in the United States where hundreds of stations cover the country. Although these stations have greater opportunity to serve the local community, to give expression to its talent, to its personalities and to its preoccupations, they have difficulty in avoiding domination by a few production centres. Because of the material and talent resources required for top telecasts, major evening programming is controlled by networks and film producers who are located almost exclusively in New York and Hollywood, with Chicago a very poor third.

International television is liable to accentuate this tendency. Pointing to this danger are, for instance, the determined efforts of the Canadian Broadcasting Corporation to prevent the domination of the Canadian audience by programmes from the United States and to develop programmes out of the resources of Canada herself, the fear in Great' Britain that commercial television will bring the importation of large quantities of foreign films, the concern of a little country like Switzerland that its national culture may be dominated by a flood of programmes from the major neighbouring countries speaking its national languages, and the growing number of foreign films used by television in Latin America.

More than ever it will have to be the concern of programme directors to make television a medium for the true expression of the thought, the aspirations and the culture of every region and every class within a nation. Their task will be more difficult when television becomes a vehicle for telecasts from countries all over the world. Major nations are likely to preserve more easily their identity in television programming and to achieve a healthy balance between regional, national and foreign programmes. Small countries will find it harder to feed sufficient high quality telecasts into this voracious medium. They will be more inclined to rely predominantly on imports from abroad.

No one who has any concern for freedom of expression, which alone can preserve and expand the rich diversity of human civilization, will consider the advent of television on the national and international level as an unmitigated boon.

While there is danger in international television, there is even greater opportunity. No medium can give a more vivid impression to the rest of mankind of the life and culture of a particular group of men. In France, city dwellers have received through television a more intimate knowledge of the French peasant, his problems, his accomplishments and his colourful personality than most of them have ever had before. When television viewers go down a coal mine or share the life of immigrants, when they visit Americans at home or roam the streets of Moscow with British musicians, they enlarge their view of the world around them.

Each individual's life is determined by a play of world-wide forces, but his personal knowledge of this world is confined to a narrow circle. Here lies a major obstacle to building a constructive, informed democracy and strengthening peace. To enlarge the individual's range of personal familiarity so that it may match the range of outside forces working upon him appears to be the basic task and problem of mass communication. Here television is called upon to play a decisive role.

Grasping our visual and auditory senses, mediating between the familiar and the strange, international television is able to link us powerfully to our fellow men. Giving expression to the people rather than seeking to dominate their thought and culture, it can perform a vital service to mankind. It is the very concept of this new medium of international communication which will determine whether television is destined to fetter the world like a chain or to tie it into a band of brotherhood.

CRITICISM IN TELEVISION

PETER BLACK

IT is important before discussing television criticism in Britain to describe first the physical aspect of the job. The television critic is a journalist who has been working during the day at collecting news and gossip about television. If he reaches home early enough he can eat his dinner in a lighted room, at a table and in the company of his family. If, as is more usual, he arrives home at about 7.30 he has time for only a cup of coffee and a biscuit, and must eat his dinner off a tray in a room dimly lit. He must also decide during which programme he can afford to relax attention sufficiently to eat. He takes notes as they occur to him, because his criticism—anything from 200 to 420 words—must be telephoned to his office by 11 p.m., so that it catches the chief edition of the next day's paper. There is no time for hunting flying thoughts.

The job is death to social life. The critic, even when he has no notice to write, must still watch if he is to keep in touch with the whole balance of television's output. He cannot invite friends to watch with him because their chatter distracts him. If he is exceptionally lucky he will have his wife watching with him; but wives tend to select their programmes and retire to another room when their interest has declined; the critic can count himself fortunate if he has the company of his dog.

Watching in solitude is a melancholy business, and in the summer, when it is still light at ten o'clock and the sounds of summer beat against the windows of the viewing-room, television has to be absorbing indeed to prevent the corners of the critic's mouth from turning down.

Unlike his colleagues of the cinema and theatre, the television critic is without the stimulus of company and without the sense of sharing an emotion with fellow-members of an audience. Unlike his colleagues, he cannot influence the success or failure of programmes, for once a programme has been given it seldom returns. Unlike his colleagues he has not the comparatively simple task of assessing a work presented to the public as commercial entertainment; he can only comment on its worth as part of the nightly menu. He is indeed a man deserving the keenest sympathy, though, as I hope to show, he is not without consolation.

Television criticism arrived a little behind the B.B.C.'s resumption of its television service in 1946, when Fleet Street could perceive that, with the return of peace, there was nothing to prevent television from developing as irresistibly as had radio twenty years earlier. In those days there were still very few television sets in use and the job was given to any reporter on the staff incautious enough to reveal an interest in it.

Criticism, in the sense of a fairly lengthy and reasoned assessment of programmes, developed slowly. Critics were also correspondents, whose duty was to supply their papers with a service of news about television; and as television grew it became news indeed, to an extent that alarmed and dismayed the B.B.C.'s Director-General.

This was the panel game era, when the slightest untoward incident was news. A lost ear-ring was news; a lost temper was news; an inadvertent " damn " from a compère was news; the collapse of a strapless dress would have been news had newspapers been able to think of a genteel synonym for breasts. Changes in panel teams were announced in type hitherto reserved for Ministerial changes. And the television critic-correspondent had to divide his mind : one half tried to store notes for his notice, the other half was alert for news, ready to pounce on any incident—at one stage even the prompting of an actor in a play was news—that fitted the fashionable definition of a news story. That definition was simple : " Anything that the public is going to talk about in the train next morning."

This was a perfectly fair and honourable policy, since newspapers become popular by reflecting their readers' interests, though many editors would agree that it was sometimes exaggerated. It was a phase of television history that writers on social affairs will one day wring a witty chapter from; and in the last analysis it was due not to the newspapers but to the circumstances in which television grew up. Interest in television was denied a choice; and the disproportionate notoriety surrounding television sprang from this single fact, that for the television audience the alternative to something was not something else, but nothing.

That era may be said to have ended when *What's My Line?*, which had been a focal point for the hysteria, ended its four-year run in the spring of 1955.

It was inevitable that during it newspapers in which criticism had to fight for space on news pages tended to regard criticism as more expendable than news. Some papers cut out criticism completely and filled a regular daily feature with interviews and gossip. Others, notably (if I may say so) the *Daily Mail*, gave regular daily space to criticism as part of a deliberate policy which believed that criticism would remain when the gossip had died away. Nowadays the balance has swung generally in favour of criticism, and the job of critic-correspondent has on several papers been turned into two jobs for two men.

I suggested earlier that the television critic has consolations for his lonely and peculiar life. It is true that, compared with his colleagues of the theatre and cinema, he appears to have little influence and less power. But the job of a critic does not end with these. There is also the obligation to reflect, sustain and increase interest in whatever medium he is writing about. It must be obvious that here the television critic can have great potential influence. The theatre critic has his public of thousands, the film critic has his of scores of thousands; but the television critic is read by hundreds of thousands, for precisely those reasons that persuade a football crowd to buy a newspaper on the way home in order to read about the match they have just seen.

There is no subject on which a writer who takes his work seriously cannot achieve some degree of influence. The opportunities open to a television critic are in direct proportion to the enormous public interest in television. To argue that, because television programmes are fleeting, criticism is useless, is to pick up the stick by the wrong end. It is because television is fleeting that criticism is so important.

A man who writes a play or a film can test his success very

simply: if he has pleased the public the play or film will run. Television has no such guide; the only immediate, independent public reaction available to television writers, producers and actors is that supplied next morning by the television critic. It is important that programme producers, who are working for the public, should have their work acknowledged. And because of the limitations of television, which make every studio production little more than a dress rehearsal, critical opinion can be, and should be, far more positive and helpful than is possible for, say, the critic of films or books.

The obligation to be constructive is pressing. Critics of other entertainment are recommending their readers to buy it or to leave it alone. When they have given their verdict, portioned out the praise and censure, they have done their job. The television critic has to go further and describe how, in his opinion, a programme could have been made better.

When one considers the enormous and varied output of television it will be seen that it is useless to expect from one man enlightened criticism of all subjects. Ideally a critic would have to be steeped in drama, films, documentaries, ballet, music, music-hall. He should be able to write with authority on all these things and on others that television has made peculiarly its own; the programmes such as panel games which depend upon the projection of personality, the outside broadcasts in which the use of words, once thought immaterial, is becoming of equal importance to the pictures.

One lifetime would be insufficient to acquire this ideal background. Practically the critic can only make the best of an impossible job. Asked to define what his approach should be I can only answer that it does not matter much as long as it is not reluctant and is ready to explain its point of view.

Reluctance will always be a danger as long as critics have to write too much and too often, and it may well be that the coming of commercial television will prove a godsend by removing artificial concentration on a single television programme. I know no critic who would not rather write two 1,000-word articles a week than one 400-word notice five nights a week.

The obligation to explain, plus the variation of programmes, forces the critic back upon the old rule which drama critics used to paste inside their hats: to decide what a programme is trying to do, whether it is doing it well or ill, whether it is worth doing.

The aim of the programme must be established because of the B.B.C.'s obligation to cater on its single service to fourteen million people. It is useless for a critic whose taste is on " B " level to complain that a programme is on " A " or " C " levels.

To decide what a programme is trying to do is easy. It is a factual matter. Assessment of performance and of value are matters of opinion, which is why the critic must not only give his opinion but state his case. Criticism that stops short at " because " is worthless; and criticism that supplies its " because " cannot but be valuable.

All critics are at times fatuous, unfair, trivial, inconsequential, and their arguments can be ludicrously wide of the mark. But if their conclusions are reasoned and coherently explained they are never negligible.

Critics are also journalists, who hold their jobs because readers find what they write interesting. The television audience is not hyper-critical; it defines good or bad as programmes liked or disliked; it is not, as a body, eager to discuss reasons, and is inclined to resent unfavourable criticism of a programme it has enjoyed. (It is worth noting that television is so personal a medium that in many homes the images acquire the status of invited guests. A critic who criticizes these guests seems to be telling readers that he doesn't think very much of the company they are keeping.) On the other hand they are generous with thanks when a critic is able to put into words the pleasure or disapproval that they have felt themselves.

There are two ways for a critic to keep on friendly terms with the readers who pay his salary. The dangerous way is to try to get inside their minds and flatter their judgment by agreeing with it. The other, and safer, is to pay them the compliment of honest thought, presented in a style as entertaining as time and temperament allow.

ADVERTISING ON TELEVISION

JOHN METCALF

IT is in television that advertising will gain its greatest victory
or suffer its greatest defeat.

Television's effectiveness as a selling medium has already
been demonstrated beyond need of further proof in the United
States. But, while it has sold and is selling goods there most
successfully, it has by no means always been so successful in
keeping public goodwill. There has been, indeed, continuing
public resentment over the banality and crudity of approach of
many commercials. Moreover, the padding of programme time
with old Westerns and third-rate wrestling bouts has done little
to improve the temper of American audiences towards the commercial's ultimate pay-off.

Here, in the United Kingdom, we are of course operating
differently. First, we have no sponsored programmes. Programmes are the responsibility of programme contractors appointed by the Independent Television Authority. At the time
of writing they are in London Associated Rediffusion, and in
Birmingham Associated Television and A.B.C. Television. You
advertise on television just as you advertise in a magazine or
a newspaper; you are responsible for the advertisement—the
commercial and the commercial only; the programme contractors are responsible for the programmes or, if you like, the
editorial content. Whatever the rights and wrongs of this
much-debated arrangement are, one thing it means is that considerably more talent is being brought to bear on the commercial than was, initially at any rate, brought to bear in America.
There, advertising agency talent tended to be concentrated on
programmes in order to get highest possible viewership for the

attached or inserted commercial. Here, agency talent from the beginning—and this talent is quite considerable—has been brought to bear solely on the commercials.

Secondly, British advertising has been able to learn a good deal from the mistakes made by American pioneers. There is a clear and universal realization that advertisers have a responsibility to the public over and above their responsibility to their shareholders to sell more goods. The typical British commercial has been designed to appeal to British taste in a decent and (as often as possible) an entertaining way. It incorporates what advertisers judge to be the better points of the American commercial, while doing its best to avoid the brashness and bounce that have caused so much irritation.

Thirdly, television advertising here has started against a background of considerable minority opposition and is competing with the B.B.C., whose programmes carry no commercials. There is, therefore, all the more need for the advertiser to make sure that he avoids giving offence. He has been, particularly in these early days of the medium, inclined to underplay his hand as far as hard selling is concerned, even though this means losing something of his impact, rather than overplay his hand and offend potential customers. He is doing his best—possibly too much—to pack his commercial with entertainment value, to make himself and his product liked, rather than relying on a simple and direct selling approach.

Trying to size up television, the advertiser and the advertising agent apply to it the classic criteria of any advertising medium: character, atmosphere, quantity and cost, tempered by the variable factors of size and position. Let's try and see it as they see it.

As far as character is concerned, they visualize what is now a local medium going national through networks quite shortly as is the case with the B.B.C. today. It is likely ultimately to cover 80 per cent. of the population in all but the remoter rural areas. And that's when it starts getting really interesting. It is a medium with sight, sound and movement. It is particularly valuable for demonstration purposes.

One problem: no fixed-time bookings are as yet allowed by the programme contractors. That is to say that you can book for sub-peak (afternoons), peak (seven to eight and after ten), or super-peak (eight to ten) times only. You can't say that you want to come on just after *Dragnet* or just before the *Palladium* show on Sunday night. All you can do is to make one of the various kinds of bookings and then leave it to the programme contractor to put your commercial where he decides. This means considerable difficulties for the advertiser both in terms of impact and merchandizing. In the development days certainly, it would seem that television is more suitable as an education and reminder medium.

It is television's atmosphere which makes it most attractive to the advertiser. He can reach his audience, relaxed and at ease, in the home; he has an unprecedented opportunity for intimate selling on a woman-to-woman or man-to-man basis.

Many advertisers believe that television is not so effective in relation to prestige and glamour products. Certainly, the home atmosphere tends to cut down any kind of phonily pretentious idea to its true size.

The Americans have already found, for example, that women react best to someone like themselves. They won't be sold a new cake-mix by someone who looks like a cross between Marlene Dietrich and Diana Dors. What does she know about it anyway? But someone who looks like the woman next door, who talks as the woman next door talks, in words that she might use, is likely to be able to convince them in a practical and common-sense way that this new cake-mix has got something to it—and really, why not try it anyway?

About quantity, the third criterion, it is too early to talk. So much depends on the quality of programmes in the development stages. Research, with all its weaknesses, is having to do the measuring. Most advertisers feel, however, that the novelty of the new medium more than counter-balances the relative sparseness of the audience, and indeed the audience is growing at a rate that makes it begin to look a really good buy by Autumn 1956.

The cost equates, of course, to the viewership. At first sight, the general impression is that the basic £650 per minute for peak time (lower for sub-peak and more expensive for super-peak) is fair in relation to the impact of a fresh advertising approach. To this must be added, of course, the production cost of the commercial itself—on an average perhaps another £200 or so if its total cost is spread over, say, four or five repetitions.

Nearly all commercials are on film. They are submitted in

173

advance to the programme contractors who clear them, under the overall supervision of the I.T.A., for subject matter, style and so on. The basic cost of commercials will rise as viewers increase. But programme contractors are confident that they will continue in a competitive relationship to comparable media like newspapers and magazines.

When you come to the variation factors of size and position new problems arise. First of all, there can be no such thing as "bigness." Newspaper spaces can be "big"—a half-page in the *Daily Express* or a whole page in the *Daily Mirror* are "big" impact spaces which play an important part in the complicated organization of an over-all advertising campaign. But on television you can only go on longer. What's more, your extra length will not give you proportionately more viewers.

So there is a diminishing return of value for extra length except in so far as length permits more intensive demonstration, more selling points, or a fuller build-up of a given atmosphere. Indeed, the extra length bought in an attempt to achieve "bigness" may well cause resentment ("What are they carrying on about?") if not properly used.

Secondly, two exceptions to the overall rule of no advertising participation in programmes have been closely studied. Semi-commercial documentaries are allowed and are indeed welcomed by programme contractors as giving them cheap programme material. These need very skilful handling to make the required impact in the goodwill domain without causing resentment. The same applies in the selling field to shopping guides, where advertisers can buy various time slices. Shopping guides, really well done, can be of considerable editorial interest and are potentially a valuable section of the whole medium.

The question of position is complicated by the no-fixed-time ruling. All that the advertiser can hope to do here is to be lucky; but if public habits are closely watched he can perhaps find himself a bargain. For example, 7.30 to 8, at the moment a peak time, is proving to be a very good spot, giving super-peak value.

These then are the mechanistic ways in which advertisers and advertising agents are looking at the new medium. But perhaps the most exciting thing about it all is the number of other, wider questions they are being forced to ask themselves. The advent of television has caused more heart-searching in the British advertising industry than any other single event. More fresh thinking has gone into the preparation of a few hundred commercials than has gone into tens of thousands of newspaper and magazine advertisements.

All this is good for the industry and good for the public by whose goodwill it lives and for whose goodwill it works. Mistakes—a lot of mistakes—are certainly being made in these early days. But the advertising industry is at least awake to its responsibilities and aware of the difficulties.

No one is going into commercial television half-heartedly. The challenge that the new medium represents has been accepted seriously and gladly. The quality of the commercials on British television screens and the success or otherwise of those commercials in British homes are the only test. Unless those commercials are successful both in terms of selling goods and creating goodwill, in a few years time there just will not be any commercial television. Perhaps the most helpful evidence of the first three months is the fact, shown by research, that, by and large, viewers have developed a real liking for the commercials themselves, entirely apart from programmes.

THE TELEVISION COMMERCIAL

THE American television commercial is a complex creative effort because at least six different persons all contribute their own ideas to the interpretation of a writer's one basic idea.

The producer and the director, the cameraman and the editor, the actor and the art director, all may add their own viewpoints to what the writer had in mind. Consequently, if the writer has not been completely clear in putting his thoughts on paper, or if the producer fails to guide the basic idea through the many phases of production, the result can become a jumble of confusion.

First of all, a clear-cut definition of the purpose and dimensions of an American television commercial is needed.

The commercial is an advertising message, of course, but perhaps its objective is made more lucid by defining it as an advertising message that should contain information of personal interest to the viewer in a highly memorable form.

This information may lie in such things as a graphic demonstration of a mechanical product in use, the appetite appeal of a food product, or the entertainment of a jingle or cartoon telling happily of the product's superiority.

Such information must, of course, be clothed in a form of personal interest to the viewer. He wants to know what the product will do for him, how it will make his way of life easier, happier and better. Information alone is not enough—it must be the particular information that wins the personal attention and interest of the viewer and creates a desire for the product (or service) advertised.

Finally, this information must be in a highly memorable form. It may be that jingle or cartoon which repeats itself in the viewer's consciousness. It may be a very graphic demonstration or an appetising scene that etches product benefits on to the viewer's mind. It may be a skilful repetition of words and pictures that makes a deeper impact on memory. To be effective, it must be remembered for its salient points long after it has been telecast—when the actual sale can be made.

The points of information of personal interest to the viewer in a highly memorable form are, in actual fact, the objectives of almost all forms of advertising. Television simply points up these three needs because it is a medium that has a greater potential for accomplishing each one. So, if television is to be used for the advertising message, use it comprehendingly.

In the United States, television commercials run as little as 10 seconds, as long as 3 minutes, with 20 and 60 seconds as the two most popular lengths. American advertisers can buy "station-break" spots between regular programmes for a message as short as 10 seconds. This takes the form of "reminder" advertising in that it is chiefly useful in supporting other advertising by repeating the product name with one simple copy point or slogan.

The 20-second spot is used between programmes, the stations generally placing both a 20- and a 10-second spot in their allotted 30 seconds of time between shows.

American advertisers also buy completed programmes, in which they use the 20- and the 60-second commercial as well as other lengths. In each 30-minute programme they are allotted 3 minutes of advertising; in each one-hour programme, 6 minutes. Sometimes in an hour programme they may use one long commercial two or three minutes in length, the other commercials being proportionately shorter. Also, within programmes, the 90-second commercial is popular.

Finally, advertisers in the United States may buy 20- or 60-second commercials in "participating" programmes. This means that a number of advertisers will all be contained within a single programme and so participate in an extended sports telecast, a feature film screening, or the like. The "participating" programme most nearly approaches the form of Britain's commercial television. The advertiser does not buy a programme but simply participates with other advertisers in the

M

overall programming of the station. American time-lengths are 7, 15, 20, 30, 60, 90 and 120 seconds in general. Actually, Britain's form of commercial television is not unlike buying advertising space in a newspaper or magazine where the advertising message must stand strictly on its own merit, must win the reader's interest, inform him and attempt to make that impression memorable. At the same time, gearing a television commercial to do its best job in the medium is rather more difficult than preparing an advertisement for a newspaper or magazine.

The ideal writer of a television commercial would be one who has experience in three fields so that he may dominate the task before him and create his script with a single, sharp perspective. He needs to be: a writer—with creative skill in graphic ideas, and the words and pictures that communicate these ideas to others; a craftsman—with experience in the techniques of film and live television, to know how best to achieve the maximum potential of the medium; an advertising man— with competent knowledge of his objectives and the place that television serves in overall selling strategy for his product.

Such a combination in one person is rare. In the United States a decade of commercial television has developed only a handful who can do this complete creative task successfully. As an alternative, the American advertising agency has come to rely on a creative team of three or more specialists to accomplish the single purpose.

This arrangement, however, is not always entirely satisfactory. There are faults when too many work on the basic writing of the commercial. The perspective may be lost. The script may have to be revised and repaired too many times and the result may be patchwork. Creatively, complete democracy is impractical. There must be one dominant figure to keep an eye on the objective and correlate the contributions of the others to a single well-defined end.

An analogy is in the cinema. Many feature pictures fail to satisfy either the theatre patrons or the box-office because of a diffusion of viewpoints. How often one hears these comments: "The director failed to interpret the writer's story"; "The actors were miscast"; "The picture was remade until it lost all sense of continuity"; "It was advertised as one thing—yet it turned out to be something different."

Feature pictures often fail because they require the creative contribution of so many people—and lack the dominant controlling figure who senses the creative spark and the objective of the story and carefully controls all effort to that one end. The producer-director, the writer-director, the single person who knows two or more phases of the complex work has a definite advantage.

This is the secret of success for a Carol Reed, a David Lean, a Cecil de Mille. They know their medium and they dominate. They know exactly what they want to do and how to accomplish it. They surround themselves with craftsmen who join them in a single objective.

Television commercial production can profit from this example of the successful cinema. But, in addition, it must also combine the advertising viewpoint and herein lies an added complexity.

In the early days of commercial television in the United States there were many competent film writers and producers who knew their own craft thoroughly but failed to understand advertising viewpoints. Similarly, competent advertising men found themselves baffled by the techniques required by this unfamiliar audio-visual medium.

Since it is difficult to get a solid grounding in the field of advertising or the field of film (or television) production in anything short of years, few people have had the opportunity to learn both well simultaneously.

It may be another decade before the ideal commercial writer develops in sufficient numbers to take care of the industry's obvious needs. In the meantime, teamwork is in order, and there are several approaches to be taken.

Three methods of team operation are: step-by-step, or assembly-line methods; agency conference and collaboration technique; agency-producer collaboration.

There are, of course, many variations of these three methods in America's three thousand advertising agencies. Some of the larger agencies produce as many as 2,500 television commercials a year, while a smaller agency may produce as few as only a dozen.

The larger agency, producing over a thousand commercials a year, has operational problems in turning out such vast quantities of creative work. Writing is only one of the problems—

the art direction and physical production, too, are important factors in the final quality.

One major agency uses the step-by-step or assembly-line method. Writers receive the assignment and prepare the commercial script, which then goes to the art director for storyboards or sketches of key scenes. The agency then submits it to the client or sponsor for approval. Finally, it goes to the film or the live production department for actual translation to the medium.

The hazards of such an operation are fairly obvious: in a creative work the perspective may be changed many times before it is finally brought to life. There is lacking the one dominant controlling figure who must keep perspective correctly focused—and be responsible for the success of the venture.

A second plan uses the simultaneous collaborative efforts of writer, art director, film (or live) television producer—all members of the agency's television department. In conference they examine the data on the assignment and discuss the possible solution to the problem before any actual writing·is done. Frequently, an account representative for the agency is present to answer questions of policy or intent. The advertising manager for the sponsor may also be present, but this is doubtful since this is an agency meeting on the mechanics rather than the strategy of the advertising.

Such conference creative work is no better than the manpower available. It does prevent the mistakes of step-by-step assembly, but the final result can be as poor as the worst member of the group rather than as good as the best.

Again, this method can often be successful if primary authority and responsibility are delegated to one man rather than the group as a whole. This one man, in most cases, most logically is the writer, since the basic creative concept is generally his. He should in turn draw on the production man for suggestions in translating his ideas to film or live television, and he should also turn to his art director for consultation on the styling and design of the commercial.

Many agencies do not have television art directors and seem to fare reasonably well without them. An experienced television art director can be most valuable, however, when he has practical experience in the medium.

Production men, for both live and film television, should be competent personnel, able to go into a studio and produce and direct. These, too, may be difficult to find because it is no small task to combine the talents of film production with a knowledgeable experience in visual advertising. Film craftsmanship alone will not accomplish the desired end, because the television commercial generally requires a different approach and different types of lighting, camera-work, direction and editing.

For instance, most commercials are in high-key lighting, bright in mood and atmosphere. Camera-work deals more in close-ups than other types of production. Special lenses and handling are often required. Direction must always consider the advertising requirements of the message, yet never insult the intelligence of the viewer. Editing, or cutting, invariably is faster in tempo and employs a great many more opticals to condense action into a shorter time limit.

A few agencies in the United States, after various organizational experiments, have finally come to the conclusion that the problem is so complex that some of the services should be purchased from outside suppliers. Since special writing, special art work and special photography are occasionally bought from outside sources, why not do the same for television commercials?

Of the thousand film production companies specializing in film commercials in the States, roughly a score now feature this creative service for the agency. They work in this way. They are supplied with the commercial problem, copy theme, market data and an indication of the desired budget, and they do the complete job, script-to-screen. The most successful film suppliers who offer this service obviously are men with advertising experience on top of their film craft background, and it has taken them ten years of television experience in the States to establish themselves in this field.

In addition to the complete creative service offered by these few producers, practically all other commercial producers offer a re-write service, whereby they will revise the agency script to make it more feasible for production and more economical in budget, without in any way changing the objective of the original idea.

It is interesting to note that, generally, the writer should have complete charge of the idea up to the point where it is to be produced and, at that time, it is often wise to give the authority to the producer, whether film or live. The reason is that production work is so complex; it is rare that a writer's ability extends to this field. Of course, it is vital that the writer completely translate his viewpoint to the producer. This is why the video instructions of a script should be crystal-clear in information, so that all concerned can carry through with the original perspective in mind.

The writer is the one man who can prevent most failures in the development of a television commercial. The detail and clarity with which his script is written holds the key to the successful interpretation by the other creative men. Each scene and each action must be described so expertly that only one clear picture is created in their minds. If the script has not told the whole story in such a way as to give the same basic mental picture to all, it has failed. The weak script that gets numerous revisions and additional material in the course of production may wind up as nothing but a hodge-podge.

The writer at all times must remember that good advertising copy is the same in all media: it should be simple, human and persuasive. Simple, easy-to-understand words make it easy to believe and hard to forget. The human factor involves the writer's psychological understanding of his viewing audience. The persuasive power is the selling job of advertising itself.

Creative writing is at all times the communication of ideas with imagination. This is true in any form of creative writing. In television, where the potential for imagery is greater and the audience itself is broader, this communication of ideas requires a special understanding of the people to be reached. Call it psychological if you will; it is partly intuitive and party schooled.

The writer must understand the viewer or the viewer will not understand the message. The writer's own taste is no criterion. He must know about his viewer, where he lives, what experiences he shares, to bridge the gap of communication.

Hazards are greater in the production of television commercials than in any other form of advertising. There is one compensating factor: you can make a great many mistakes and still be successful because television has an impact greater than anything advertising has ever known before. The tremendous potential of the medium is still unrealized because the television commercial, as we know it today, is undoubtedly only in its adolescence.

GLOSSARY

TELEVISION AND FILM TERMS

THE terms given in this glossary are those in general use in English-speaking countries. Wherever terms are more commonly or wholly associated with American television, this is indicated. Where British terms have an American equivalent, these are also given by cross-reference.

A. ACOUSTIC PERSPECTIVE. An apparent spatial relationship between different sources of sound.

ACOUSTICS. The science of sound, particularly as applied to the design of concert halls, broadcasting, television and film studios, and microphones; the acoustic properties of an enclosed space. Hence *acoustic treatment*, the application of material to the walls, ceilings, floor or furnishings of e.g., a studio, for the purpose of modifying its acoustic properties by the absorption or reflection of sound waves.

ACOUSTIC SCREEN. A movable screen having absorbent or reflecting surfaces, or both, used to produce local variations in the acoustics of a studio or of a location in which sound is being recorded for transmission.

ADLUX (American trade-name). A photo-transparency lit from behind for giving illusion of illuminated signs or for miniature displays.

AERIAL. An arrangement of conductors, or other electrical elements, supported at a height above the ground for the purpose of either radiating or of collecting electro-magnetic waves for radio or television.
Hence: (1) *Anti-fading aerial*, a transmitting aerial for use on medium wave-lengths designed to reduce fading by confining the radiation as far as possible to a low elevation so as to reduce the strength of indirect waves and thus to reduce the extent to which they interfere with direct waves. (2) *Directional aerial*, a transmitting aerial designed to radiate waves in some directions more effectively than in others; a receiving aerial designed to collect waves from some directions more effectively than from others. (3) *Frame aerial*, a directional aerial consisting of a number of turns of wire coiled on a vertical frame. See *Antenna* (American).

AMBIENT LIGHT. Overall level of light in a studio not directed specifically at any particular object or scene.

AMPLIFIER. An apparatus designed to produce, by means of power drawn from a local electrical source, an electrical output that is greater than and bears a prescribed (usually linear) relationship to the input.

AMPLITUDE MODULATION. See *Modulation*.

ANGSTROM UNIT. Unit of measurement to express length of light waves. Used also to define colour values obtainable from different kinds of illumination sources.

ANIMATE. To film static drawings or objects (e.g., puppets) by stop-motion (one frame exposed at a time) so that when the finished film is projected an illusion is produced of continuous movement. Hence *animation bench, animated cartoon, animated diagram.* See also *Stop-motion.*

ANNOUNCER. Male or female personality who introduces a television programme or series of programmes. (Mainly used by the B.B.C. and some European television stations.)

ANSWER PRINT (American). See *Grading Print.*

ANTENNA (American). See *Aerial.*

ARC. Arc-lamp. A high-intensity type of light widely used in film production.

ART DIRECTOR. Technician who designs studio sets (and sometimes costumes) and supervises construction of same for television programmes or films.

ARTIFICIAL BARS (*abbrev.* Art. Bars). A still pattern for testing purposes in the form of a black cross on a white background, produced by electronic means without the use of a television camera.

ASPECT RATIO. The ratio of the breadth of a televised picture to its height; in the B.B.C. system, a ratio of four wide to three high.

ATMOSPHERE. The sounds forming the audible background incidental to an event such as a race-meeting, procession, etc. Hence *atmosphere microphone,* a microphone specially placed to pick up such sounds; also microphones placed to respond to reflected sound in a studio so as to enable variations to be made in the acoustic background.

AUDIMETER (American). An electro-mechanical attachment to a television or radio set to record when it is in use and to what channel or station it is tuned.

AUDIO FREQUENCY. See *Frequency.*

B.

BACK-PROJECTION. A system of projecting a picture, either a static photograph or a moving film, on to a translucent screen behind a studio set and photographing the resulting effect on film or television, thus giving the impression that the studio set is located within the surroundings portrayed in the projected picture. See *Rear-projection* (American).

BACKING. One or more flats placed beyond an opening in scenery or set. Hence *door backing, window backing, fireplace backing,* etc.

BAFFLE. A screen of rigid material used to increase the length of the path of sound waves between the front and the back of a loudspeaker so as to improve the radiation of sound at low audio frequencies; flat baffle. Also *box baffle,* a baffle in the form of a box, lined with sound-absorbing material to damp out the natural resonance of the cavity.

BALOP (American *abbrev.*). Slang term for Balopticon (trade-name), a picture projector used in television to throw an image, usually by reflected light, of inanimate objects or photographs on to the television tube for transmission. See also *Telop* (American).

BARN DOOR. Slang term for an adjustable fitting applied to an illuminator to produce a beam of rectangular cross-section, the dimensions of which can be varied.

188

BEL. Unit of sound measurement; equal to the logarithm of the ratio between two powers measured at the same impedance.

BIG-SCREEN TV. See *Projection-TV*.

BILLING. (1) Name credit on the screen at the beginning or end of a television programme or film. (2) Name credit used in printed publicity about a programme (e.g., announcements in the *Radio Times* or other such journal).

BLACK LEVEL. The datum line, in the transmitted wave-form representing a vision signal, from which (in the B.B.C. system) picture signals start in a positive sense and synchronizing signals in a negative sense.

BLAST. Overloading of camera or sound equipment causing a sudden distortion.

BLIMP. A sound-proof case in which a film camera or film projector is placed in order to prevent the noise of its mechanism from being picked up by a microphone.

BLOCKING SHOTS (American). Slang term for breaking down action as described in the script into separate camera shots, or set-ups, sometimes done on the studio-floor at first rehearsal.

BLOOP. Slang term for an opaque patch painted, cemented or printed on to the sound track of film over a join (or splice) to prevent an audible click being reproduced as the join interrupts the reproducing light-beam in the projector. Always applied to sound tracks before re-recording or mixing.

BLUE LIGHTING. Lighting produced by mercury discharge lamps. See *Cold Lighting*, also *Lighting*.

BLUE PRINT. See *Fine-grain Print*.

BOOM. Long, movable (sometimes extendible) arm for suspending microphone in mid-air and allowing it to be moved from one position to another during the taking of a shot. Hence operator known as *boom-man*, *boom-swinger*.

BOOSTER STATION. A subsidiary television transmitting station that takes vision signals by direct radio reception from a main station and rebroadcasts them on the same frequency channel as that used by the main station. See also *Satellite Station*.

BOX SET. A studio set using four-wall construction of a room with actual openings for doors, windows, etc.

BRACE. A strut to hold up scenery or flats. Hence *French brace*, a strut permanently attached, usually by means of a hinge, to a piece of scenery or a flat.

BREAKDOWN. A detailed analysis of a television or film script listing camera set-ups, cast, scene numbers, sets, properties, locations, materials, etc. See *Blocking Shots* (American).

BRIGHTNESS. The amount of light reflected by, or produced by, a surface per unit of area.

BROADSIDE. A form of small floodlighting unit. Also slang term: *broad*.

BUZZ-TRACK. Slang term for *unmodulated track*.

C. CABLE. An insulated conductor or group of conductors, separately insulated and laid up together, usually provided with a protective covering. Hence: (1) *Balanced-pair cable:* a cable containing one or more pairs of conductors, each pair comprising two similar wires so arranged as to be electrically symmetrical with respect to earth. (2) *Coaxial cable:* a cable containing one or more pairs of conductors, at least one pair comprising an inner conductor surrounded by, but separated from, a concentric tube forming the second conductor. Coaxial cable is used for television transmission over distances because of its low loss of power at the higher video frequencies.

CABOT'S QUILT. A sound-absorbing material consisting of dried seaweed sewn between layers of canvas.

CALL LETTERS (American). Initials assigned by the Federal Communications Commission of the U.S. Government to identify a television station, which must be announced or shown together with the channel number at least once every half-hour. See also *Station Break.*

CALL-SHEET. Schedule of daily shooting, stating time to check-in for cast, time to be made-up and for reporting for work on studio set or location.

CAMERA CARD. Extract from a television camera script, usually typed in abbreviated form on a small card, containing information of a technical nature required for the operation of one specific camera.

CAMERA CUE. Light, usually red, on front or on top of a television camera, lit only when the camera is on transmission. Known also as a *tally light.*

CAMERA SCRIPT. The text of a television script with full technical details for studio staff and director. See also *Script.*

CAMERA SET-UP. Position in which a television or film camera is placed for a required shot.

CAMERA TUBE. An electronic tube used in a television camera.

CANS. Slang term for headphones worn by television cameramen, stage-manager or other technicians as required on the studio-floor, or on location, so that they can receive the producer's or director's instructions without the rest of the staff and cast hearing.

CAPTION. (1) A printed or hand-lettered statement shown on the viewing screen, not forming part of a scene but for the purpose of conveying to the audience information necessary for the understanding of a programme. (2) Also used synonymously with *title.* See also *Credits, Title.*

CARTOON. See *Animate.*

CATHODE-RAY TUBE. A sealed vessel, usually funnel-shaped and made of glass, containing a high vacuum and enclosing a system of electrodes designed to produce a beam of electrons and to project it on to the fluorescent screen which constitutes the inner surface at the wide end of the tube, thus producing a bright spot which can be focussed on the screen and deflected to any part of it. Hence *picture tube,* a cathode-ray tube used in a television receiver to display the pictures.

CHANGE-OVER. The point at which one reel of film ends on a projector and the next begins. An instantaneous change from one projector to the other is necessary to secure uninterrupted projection. Special punch-marks made at the laboratory in the film give the operator the cues to change.

CHANNEL. Electrical or electro-magnetic path (such as a circuit, line or radio-link) for a television programme output. Frequently used with numbers to denote which station output is being received on a television set.

CIRCUIT. (1) The closed path for an electric current. (2) A network of such paths in a piece of electrical equipment. Hence: (1) *Closed circuit:* a channel for testing, rehearsal, or other purpose not involving telecast transmission. See also *Reproduction.* (2) *Feed-back circuit:* a circuit by which the personnel at a programme source can hear (usually for cueing purposes) a programme originating elsewhere. (3) *Talk-back circuit:* a circuit enabling spoken directions to be given from a studio control-room, or a mobile control-room, for the purpose of directing a performance or rehearsal. See *Speak-back,* also *Talk-back.*

CLAPPER-BOARD. A number board with clappers attached thereto. See also *Number Board.*

CLAPPERS. Two boards hinged together at one end and used to make a clap or bang in front of a film camera, thus producing a pronounced modulation on the sound track which, when related on a synchronizer to the first of the sequence of pictures showing the boards in contact with one another, enables the sound-cutting point and the picture-cutting point to be synchronized for the purpose of editing. Hence *clapper-boy,* the member of the camera staff who operates the clappers and marks them according to the script.

CLIP (American). A shot or sequence of shots cut or " clipped " from a complete film to be used in a television or film programme as an insert. See also *Stock Shot.*

CLOSED CIRCUIT. See *Circuit.*

COATED LENS. A lens of a television or film camera the surface of which has been treated to reduce reflection and thus to increase the amount of light transmitted through it on to the negative film.

COAXIAL. See *Cable.*

COLD LIGHTING. The illumination produced by discharge lamps in which the ratio of heat to light produced is much less than in lamps containing incandescent filaments. See also *Blue Lighting, Lighting.*

COLOUR RESPONSE. Of a television camera tube, the output in relation to the colour of the light to which it is exposed.

COMBINED PRINT. The positive print of a film carrying both sound and picture in synchronization, the sound being printed 19 frames ahead of the picture on 35 mm. and 26 frames ahead on 16 mm. Known also as a *married* or *synchronized print.*

COMMENTATOR. See *Narrator.*

COMMERCIAL. Loosely, the advertising message either (1) integrated into a television programme or inserted at the beginning, middle and/or end (American system—slang term *spot*); or (2) added as a short item preceding or following or in a natural break in a programme but separate from it (British system). Hence *commercial television* as distinct from television as a public service financed by licence fees, taxes on sales of receivers, or government subsidy.

COMPATIBILITY. Reception in black-and-white pictures on a monochrome television receiver of colour transmission without alteration to the set. Conversely, reception of a black-and-white picture on a colour television receiver without adaptation of the set.

CONDENSER. A device for storing electricity consisting of two conductors separated by an insulator (dielectric).

CONSOLE. See *Control Desk*.

CONTINUITY. The process of carrying the attention of an audience viewing a television programme or a film smoothly from one shot or sequence of shots to the next without any displeasing, illogical break or sense of incongruity. Lapses of time and changes of place are made by *continuity devices*, such as *dissolves* (or *mixes*) and *fades*. Hence *continuity girl*, a secretary in film-making who is responsible for noting the details of every take during shooting in order to ensure that no discrepancies occur to disturb smooth continuity of action, words, clothes, etc., when the shots come to be edited together in their proper order.

CONTINUOUS MOTION. An even movement of a film, e.g., in a telecine or telerecording machine, as distinct from an intermittent movement from frame to frame.

CONTRAST. The variation between tones either in a scene or in a picture. Hence *contrast range*, the ratio of the brightness of the brightest tone to that of the darkest tone.

CONTROL DESK or PANEL. (1) A table designed for the operational control of technical equipment; for example, in a control-room adjacent (usually overlooking) a television studio, a desk fitted with panels carrying controls for sound and picture that enable a producer or director, assisted by technicians, to mix and cut the outputs of picture and sound from the studio floor, to mix in other sound effects from discs, to insert film sequences from telecine, and to give cues and spoken instructions to technicians and cast in the studio. (2) At a transmitting station, a desk fitted with panels carrying controls and instruments which enable an engineer to start up a transmitter and supervise its performance. (3) In film recording, the control panel used for recording, re-recording, etc., is usually known as a *console*.

CONTROL-ROOM. A room, usually adjacent to and often overlooking a television studio, in which the artistic and operational direction of a programme is carried out on the control desk. For outside broadcasts, a travelling van is used, known as a *mobile control-room*. The room in which the selection, switching and supervision of a series of television programmes is conducted is known as a *central control-room*.

CRAB. Slang term for a three-legged, folding device on which to stand a television or film camera tripod to prevent it from slipping.

CRANE SHOT. Shot taken by a television or film camera mounted at the end of a crane arm so that it can be moved through space, usually on an electrically-controlled dolly. See *Dolly*.

CREDITS or CREDIT TITLES. Titles placed at the beginning or end of a television programme or film bearing the names of the cast, the main technicians and company responsible for the production. See also *Billing, Caption, Title*.

CREEPING TITLE. A title which is moved slowly up the television or film screen, usually operated by a roller-drum device. Also known as a *crawling title* (American) or a *roller title*.

CROSS-CUT. To cut alternately from one shot to another in the editing of a film, or from one camera to another in transmitting a television programme, so that sections of each are seen successively. See also *Parallel development*.

CROWFOOT (American). See *Crab*.

CUE. A prearranged signal to a studio or other programme source for the starting or finishing of a programme or part of a programme. Hence: (1) *Hand cue*, a cue given by gesture, often by the stage-manager to actors or others taking part in a television programme. (2) *Light cue*, a cue given by means of a light, usually green; a flick.

CUT. (1) To delete a word or passage from a script or television programme. (2) To terminate suddenly the output of a channel. (3) To change over instantaneously from one television picture channel to another. (4) To terminate a film shot by instructing the cameraman and sound recordist to stop the cameras at the end of a take. (5) The transition between two film shots linked by a simple join, giving the impression to an audience that the first shot is instantaneously displaced by the second. Hence *cutting* is often used synonymously with *editing*. (6) In recording, to lower the cutting stylus on to the surface of a disc and to make in the coating of a disc the spiral groove that constitutes the sound track.

CUT-KEY. (1) A switch provided for the purpose of enabling the output of a microphone to be interrupted. Hence *microphone cut-key*. (2) A switch provided for the purpose of changing instantaneously from one television picture channel to another.

CUTTING-COPY. The picture and sound-tracks of a film in its penulti-mate stage, usually with opticals, titles, etc., inserted (or at least indicated) but still before negative cutting. See *Work-print* (American).

CUTTING-ROOM. A room, complying with official safety regulations, sometimes adjacent to a film or television studio, where the process of editing and track-laying a film is performed. Vaults for film storage are normally attached.

CYCLE. The complete formation of a wave from zero, through peak and valley, and back to zero.

CYCLORAMA. A semi-circular backcloth, or screen, encircling the rear of the studio stage, used to suggest sky or neutral backing.

D. DECIBEL. A unit of measurement of sound volume; one-tenth of a bel.

DEFINITION. The degree of fineness of detail in a television picture.

DENSITOMETER. Apparatus for measuring the density of film.

DENSITY. A measure of a film's power of transmission. Equal to the logarithm of its opacity, or the logarithm of the reciprocal of its transmission.

DEPTH OF FOCUS. The range of distances from a camera lens within which every point in a scene appears to be in focus, this range being dependent on the aperture at which the lens is set; depth of field.

DEVELOP. To treat a photographic emulsion coated on film stock with chemicals so that the latent image is turned into metallic silver and consequently rendered opaque.

DIAPHRAGM. The thin plate of a microphone which receives the wave front.

DIFFUSER. (1) A translucent sheet of silk, gelatine, frosted glass, or other suitable material placed in front of a studio lamp to soften and diffuse its light. (2) A similar device placed in front of a camera lens to soften the outlines of the picture. Hence *diffusion disc.* See also *Jelly, Scrim.*

DIORAMA. Miniature replica used in model-work to give an illusion of a large location impracticable or too costly to erect in the studio.

DIRECTIONAL AERIAL. See *Aerial.*

DIRECTOR. The controlling, creative individual in charge of a television programme or film, who co-operates with the script-writer, directs the actors and their action, approves the settings and (in film) supervises the editing. In television, he directs the programme on transmission from the control-room, giving directions when to cut from camera to camera, when to insert film sequences and sound effects, etc. Note: In the B.B.C. Television Service, directors are most frequently called Producers, a practice that gives rise to considerable confusion both within and without the Corporation. See also *Producer.*

DIRECT WAVE. An electro-magnetic wave that, on leaving a transmitting aerial, travels directly to a receiving aerial.

DISSOLVE or MIX. The fade-out of one picture and the fade-in of another picture superimposed on each other for an equal length of time. In television, the device is obtained by use of two cameras; in film, it is made in the laboratory by an optical printer. See also *Optical.*

DISTRIBUTOR. A piece of rotating electrical machinery which supplies a number of motors with current so arranged that they all rotate synchronously.

DOLLY. A movable trolley on four wheels, sometimes electrically controlled, to carry a television or film camera and operator which can be steered about the set or location as desired while shooting.

DOUBLE-EXPOSURE. Two pictures superimposed one on top of the other on the same film negative or television screen. See also *Superimposition.*

DOUBLE-HEADED PROJECTION. The projection of picture and sound track of a film separately but in synchronization on a special type of projector, at "rushes," assembly or later stage of editing before negatives are cut and a combined print is obtainable.

DOUBLE-SYSTEM. Using a film camera to take the pictures required on one negative and a second camera to record sound on another negative to go with same, both cameras running in synchronization by electric motor. See also *Single-system.*

DRAPES. Curtains used for background in a studio.

DROIT MORAL (Legal term). The right of a copyright owner in some countries to prohibit any use of his work which might be prejudicial to his honour or reputation.

DROITS VOISONS (Legal term). Rights analogous or ancillary to copyright, e.g., the rights of broadcasting or television organizations, record manufacturers and artistes in material broadcast or telecast, recorded or performed by them.

DRY-RUN. Pre-transmission television rehearsal prior to camera rehearsal where action, lines, cues, etc., are tried out and perfected.

DUB. Slang term for: (1) Re-recording the sound track of a film, substituting for the original speech a spoken translation in another language. (2) Transferring recorded sound material from one recording to another; hence *re-record, dubbing*. See also *Re-record, Mix* (sound).

DUPE NEGATIVE. See *Duplicate Negative*.

DUPING PRINT. See *Fine-grain Print*.

DUPLICATE NEGATIVE. A second negative made from a positive print specially processed for the purpose, known as a *fine-grain duplicating print*, a *blue print*, *lavender* or *master positive*. Slang: *dupe negative*.

E.

ECHO. (1) The repetition of a sound after an interval of time, caused, for example, by reflection of sound waves or by the propagation of electro-magnetic waves over more than one path. (2) Reverberation artificially added to the output from a studio or hall. Hence *echo room, echo chamber*, a reverberant room, containing only a loudspeaker and a microphone, through which an output from a studio or hall is passed in order to allow a variable degree of reverberation to be added to the direct output from the same source.

EDGE-NUMBERS. Identifying letters and numbers printed by the manufacturers on film stock at 1-foot intervals to identify frames and shots and sound tracks during editing and negative cutting. Known also as *key-numbers*.

EDITING. The assembly of film shots and sound tracks in correct order according to the script, but also according to their appropriate length and rhythm. Editing is sometimes referred to as " cutting," but a cutter is usually a technician who does the manual part of the editing process at the editor's instructions.

EDITING MACHINE. An apparatus used during film editing to project the picture in small-scale and to reproduce sound tracks. Colloquially known by trade names, e.g., Moviola, Editola, Acmeola, etc.

ELECTRO-MAGNETIC WAVE. Mode of propagation of electric and magnetic disturbances through space (e.g., radio waves, light waves).

EMULSION. The light-sensitive coating applied to celluloid base of the film stock.

EQUALIZER. An apparatus designed to compensate for attenuation, distortion or phase distortion introduced by lines or equipment. Hence: (1) *Bode equalizer*, an attenuation equalizer so designed that the operation of a simple control varies the amount of equalization introduced at all frequencies within its range in the same proportion. (2) *Derivative equalizer*, an equalizer designed to sharpen the detail in a television picture by simultaneously compensating for variations of both attenuation and phase.

ESTABLISHING SHOT. A long-shot introduced, usually at the beginning of the scene, to establish the inter-relationship of details subsequently shown in closer shots.

EXCHANGE PROGRAMME. A programme jointly undertaken by two or more television organizations, each contributing part of the programme material and each televising the whole programme from one or more of its stations.

EXCITER LAMP. The lamp in a sound-reproducing machine whose light is focused on to the photo-electric cell. It is the interruption of this light by the varying opacity of the film which causes variations in the output of the cell and thus results in sound from the loudspeakers.

EXPOSURE. The submission of an emulsion on film stock to light.

EXPOSURE LAMP. The lamp which provides the light exposing the negative film for sound-recording.

EXPOSURE METER. See *Photometer*, *Light Meter*.

EXTRA. An actor engaged by the day to appear in a film or television programme either in a non-speaking part or in a part where he speaks only in unison with others.

F.

FADE. (1) Sound: to change gradually the volume of the output of a channel. (2) Picture: to change gradually the intensity of a picture, either film or television, from light to dark or the reverse. Hence *fade-up*, *fade-down*, *fade-in*, *fade-out*.

FEED-BACK. Whining distortion in a loudspeaker caused by a kick-back of sound waves from one element (such as amplifier or speaker) to a prior element (such as a microphone).

FEED-BACK CIRCUIT. See *Circuit*.

FILAMENT. The electrode in a directly heated thermionic valve which, when heated, emits electrons.

FILMSTRIP. A piece of 35 mm. positive film about 3 to 4 foot in length, each frame of which bears a different image of various objects. Projected in a small machine, one picture stationary at a time, it is a useful aid in visual education and is used in television production.

FILTER. (1) Optical glass or gelatine slide which, when placed before the camera lens, corrects the colour balance or the amount of light being received through the lens. (2) A device for reducing, within a given region, the passage of sound wave formation.

FINE-GRAIN PRINT. A positive film made with special fine-grain emulsion from which a duplicative negative can be struck with a minimum loss of quality. Because the stock used sometimes has a blue base, a fine-grain print is often known as a *lavender* or *blue print*. Known also as *duping print* and *master positive*.

FLARE. See *Halation*.

FLAT. A piece of scenery, usually of wood, of appropriate height and width and as thin as construction allows. Hence *book-flat*, a pair of flats joined together by a vertical hinge so that they stand without other support.

FLIPPER. A flat secured by a hinge which enables it to be swung clear when out-of-shot in order to permit additional camera set-ups or movement which it would otherwise obstruct.

FLOAT. A piece of scenery placed in position for specific shots only. Also *floater*.

FLOATS. (1) Footlights. (2) Section of the footlight batten.

FLOOR. The area in a studio where a television programme or a film is produced; sometimes known as a *stage*.

FLOOR-MANAGER (American). See *Stage-manager*.

FLOOR PLAN. Scale plan of studio floor, or stage, in which area a television programme or film is to be produced, with locations of walls, sets, doors, exits, working areas marked. An essential for the producer or director and cameraman to work out action of scenes, camera set-ups, placing of sets, etc., prior to rehearsals or set-building.

FLUTTER. (1) Rapid fluctuation in the intensity of a sound. (2) A rapid variation of frequency in the reproduction of recorded sound caused by a cyclic irregularity in the speed of the recording or re-producing apparatus, the audible fluctuations so produced being too rapid to be recognizable as a variation of pitch. See also *Wow*. (3) Fluctuation in the brightness of a picture on the screen of a tele-vision receiver caused by reflection of the signal from a moving object, e.g., an aircraft.

FLYING-SPOT PROJECTOR. A motion-picture projector for televising film in which the light source is provided by a cathode-ray tube spot which scans the continuously moving film; the light passed by the film is picked up by a photo-electric cell which generates a video signal.

FOCUS. See *Depth of Focus*.

FOCUS PULL. The action of altering focus on a camera lens from foreground to background, or vice versa, as the point of interest changes. Hence *focus puller*, an assistant film cameraman.

FOLLOW FOCUS. See *Focus Pull*.

FOOT-CANDLE. A unit of measurement of light intensity.

FOOTAGE. A term to indicate the length of a piece of film; in English-speaking countries measured in feet, elsewhere in metres. A standard reel of 35 mm. film contains approximately 1,000 feet. A standard reel of 16 mm. film contains about 400 feet. The average running-time of a reel is 11 minutes.

FOOTAGE INDICATOR. (1) A counter situated either beside the screen or on a re-recording panel (or console) which indicates the distance from the start of a reel of film at any given moment. (2) Attached to a film camera for the same purpose. (3) Used in the cutting-room for the measurement of film.

FREQUENCY. The rate of vibration of an oscillation, measured by the number of complete cycles performed in one second. (The frequency of an electro-magnetic wave, in cycles per second, multiplied by its wave-length in metres, equals the velocity of electro-magnetic waves, including those of light, i.e., in free space, three hundred metres per second.) Hence: (1) *Audio-frequency*, the rate of oscillation corresponding to that of sound audible to the normal human ear (i.e., within the range of about sixteen cycles per second to about fifteen thousand cycles per second). (2) *Radio-frequency*, the frequency within the range (from about fifteen kilocycles per second to about ten thousand megacycles per second) in which radiation of electro-magnetic waves for radio-communication is possible. (3) *Video-frequency*, the frequency of any component of the electric signal produced by a television scanning device.

FREQUENCY MODULATION. See *Modulation*.

G. **GAIN.** (1) The extent to which an amplifier is able to increase the amplitude of a given signal. The ratio of output energy to input energy. (2) Of an aerial, the ratio of the power radiated to the power that would be radiated (other things being equal) by a standard reference aerial.

GALVANOMETER. In film-recording, a device which produces a mechanical oscillation when subjected to an alternating current; usually fitted with a mirror which reflects an oscillating light beam from a stationary light source.

GAMMA. The degree of contrast attained in a photographic film image. May be defined as the slope of the straight-line portion of the H. and D. curve.

GATE. The part of a film camera or projector in which each frame or picture is held momentarily, and through which it passes during exposure or projection.

GENLOCK. System for interlocking synchronous generators between a television outside broadcast and the studio in which the other part of the programme is being produced.

GOBO. Slang term for an opaque black screen serving, for example, to keep unwanted light from a camera lens. See also *Nigger*.

GRADING PRINT. First composite synchronized print of a finished film to be made by the laboratory, not usually graded for best photographic quality but used to correct future prints. See *Answer print* (American).

GRANDS DROITS (Legal term). Performing rights in operatic and dramatic musical works.

GRID. An electrode in a thermionic valve placed between the anode and the cathode so that variations in the potential applied to it control the flow of electrons from cathode to anode.

GROUND NOISE. (1) Noise reproduced from a sound track owing to film grain, dust, scratches, etc., or the inherent noise of the system. (2) Unmodulated sound track used for intercutting with recorded tracks to preserve a uniform background. See also *Unmodulated Track*.

GROUND WAVE. An electro-magnetic wave that is propagated over the surface of the earth from a transmitting aerial to a receiving aerial.

GUIDE-TRACK. A sound track, usually of dialogue, recorded during the shooting of a film to serve as a guide during post-synchronization and not for use in the finished film.

H.

H. & D. CURVE. The characteristic curve of a film emulsion under a given development condition. It illustrates graphically the density obtained from any given exposure. (Hurter & Driffield.)

HALATION. Light caught direct in lens of television or film camera causing a flare, often appearing as bright circle of light in picture.

HAND PROPS. Movable properties on a set in studio, or on location, used by actors in the course of their performance; also any small articles used to dress the set. See also *Properties*.

HEADROOM. (1) The area from the top of an actor's head to the height of the set. (2) Used to describe the distance on the actual screen between the top of an actor's head and the top margin of the screen.

HIGH-HAT. Slang term for a low mounting for a film camera in the form of a vertical cylinder with a flange, used for taking very low angle set-ups. Known also as *top-hat*.

HIGHLIGHT. The part of a scene that reflects the brightest light; the representation of it in a television picture or film shot. See also *Lighting*.

HORSE OPERA (American). Slang term for television programmes mainly given over to gunplay, fist-fights, chases, etc., with little vestige of plot, character or real story.

I. ICONOSCOPE. A television camera pick-up tube used before the Image Orthicon tube was perfected but needing stronger light than the latter. Used mainly today for pick-up in film projection cameras.

IDIOT SHEET (American). Slang term to describe cue sheets or script pages placed in front of the television or film camera below or beside the lens to prompt performers, announcers, public speakers, etc. See also *Teleprompter*.

IMAGE ORTHICON. An extra-light-sensitive television camera tube used widely in production.

INDUCTANCE. A unit such as a choke-coil which provides a magnetic opposition to any growth or decay of current. The measure of such opposition.

INLAY. An electro-optical method of combining in one complete television picture selected areas of two pictures obtained from separate sources, the required areas of each picture being determined by the shape and position of an opaque mask placed in a silhouette generator.

INSERT. Slang term to describe a close-up of an inanimate object, usually carrying reading matter, such as a letter, a newspaper clipping, a photograph, appearing among other shots in a television programme or film.

INTERLOCK. (1) To place three-dimensional scenery in front of a back-projection screen in such a way that it appears to be a continuation of the scene depicted on the back-projection screen. (2) A device used to synchronize two film projectors so that they run at identical speed.

IONOSPHERIC WAVE. An electro-magnetic wave that is propagated from a transmitting aerial by way of the ionosphere; reflected wave; indirect wave.

J. JELLY. Slang term for a gelatine diffuser. See also *Diffuser*.

JIB. The arm of a crane-dolly. See also *Dolly*.

K. KEY LIGHT. The main source of illumination in a scene, to which all other lights are related. See also *Lighting*.

KEY-NUMBERS. See *Edge-numbers*.

KILOWATT (*abbrev.* Kw.). A practical unit of electrical power; a thousand watts.

KINESCOPE (American). Process of filming a television programme directly off the television tube, either on 35 mm. or 16 mm. film, to be used either for a repeat showing or for post-transmission analysis. See also *Telerecording*.

L. LAVENDER PRINT. See *Fine-grain Print*.

LAZY ARM. Slang term for a small microphone-boom allowing limited movement of the microphone during operation.

199

LEADER. Blank film attached to the beginning or end of reel of film : (1) To allow it to be threaded-up in a projector so that it can run up-to-speed before the first scene appears; (2) at the end of a reel, to protect last scene from being scratched and to allow for change-over.

LENS TURRET. Revolving mounting on front of television or film camera carrying two or more lenses to permit rapid change from one lens to another.

LEVEL. (1) The intensity of a continuous tone used for test purposes (usually measured in decibels by comparison with a standard reference level, sometimes called " zero level "). Hence *level test*. (2) The intensity of a programme output or of noise; volume. See also *Black Level*.

LIBRARY MATERIAL or LIBRARY SHOT. See *Stock Shot*.

LIGHTING. The action of illuminating a scene or shot, or the extent of illumination of same, in a television programme or film. Hence : (1) *Back lighting*, lighting, usually from concentrated sources, applied from behind an object, which is thus given a sharply defined outline against its background. (2) *Flat lighting*, that which gives a substantially uniform illumination of a scene, thus giving an impression in the resulting picture of a lack of depth in the scene. (3) *Foundation lighting*, general lighting sufficient to produce a television or film picture but not usually producing by itself an artistic effect. (4) *Front lighting*, lighting of a scene or part of a scene from the front, usually achieved by means of illuminators of low power placed above or beside the camera and giving a diffused light. (5) *Hard lighting*, lighting from concentrated source which causes objects in a scene to cast sharply defined shadows so that high light and shadow are strongly contrasted. (6) *High-key lighting*, that which illuminates a scene so that the resulting television or film picture is predominantly of light tones. (7) *Low-key lighting*, that which illuminates a scene so that the resulting picture is predominantly composed of dark tones. (8) *Soft lighting*, lighting from diffused sources which results in an absence of strong shadows. See also *Ambient Lighting, Cold Lighting, High Light, Key Light, Modelling Light, Spot Light*.

LIGHTING SUPERVISOR. Technician in charge of lighting a television programme in the studio or on location. Also *lighting cameraman* (films).

LIGHT METER. See *Photometer*.

LIGHT VALVE. An electro-magnetic device for controlling the passage of light in variable density recording.

LIP-SYNCH. Slang term for direct recording of speech by actors at the same time as picture is being filmed.

LIVE TELEVISION. Term used to signify a programme or telecast being received instantaneously on a receiver as it is being enacted in the studio or on location, as distinct from a televised film or recording.

LOAD. (1) The impedance connected to the output of a piece of electrical apparatus. (2) The power consumed or delivered by some electrical machine.

LOCATION. Any exterior place, away from the studio, where action is being televised or filmed. See also *Outside Broadcast, Remote*.

LOOP. (1) Slack film left above and below the gate in a film projector or camera so as to prevent the intermittent claw-system from straining or tearing the film. (2) A length of sound track joined into a continuous band so that it can be run without cessation on a projector giving a constant sound; used largely in dubbing and re-recording. (3) A picture loop for projection on telecine (e.g., fog effect).

LOUDSPEAKER. An electro-magnetic device for converting electrical impulses into mechanical vibrations and thence into sound waves.

M. MAGAZINE. A combination of two light-proof boxes designed to permit unexposed film to pass out of one box and exposed film, having passed through the gate of the camera, to be wound into the other box.

MARKER LIGHT. A light for exposing synchronizing points on sound and picture films simultaneously.

MARRIED PRINT. See *Combined Print, Synchronized Print.*

MASK. A shield placed before a camera lens to mask off a part of the field of view.

MASTER POSITIVE. See *Fine-grain Print.*

MATTE or MATT. A specially prepared length of film run through an optical printer, together with the film to be printed, in order to mask a portion of it, thus preventing that portion from being printed. Used for trick-work.

MECHAU TELECINE PROJECTOR. A motion-picture projector for televising film in which light, normally from an incandescent source, is focused on to a continuously moving film through a series of rotating mirrors mounted on a drum which compensate for the film movement; the film image is projected through mirrors on the opposite side of the drum into a normal television camera, where it is scanned to produce a video signal. See also *Flying-Spot Projector.*

MEMORY RETENTION. A static image burnt into an Image Orthicon camera-tube as a result of it being focused on a stationary object for some thirty seconds. The image may remain several minutes unless destroyed by pointing the camera lens at a bright light, throwing the lens out of focus, or waving the camera swiftly from side to side.

MICROPHONE. An instrument by which sound waves are converted into mechanical vibrations in an alternating current. Slang term, *mike.* Hence: (1) *Carbon microphone,* dependent for its operation on the changing resistance of a pile of carbon granules as they are acted on by sound waves. (For quality work now obsolete.) (2) *Cardioid microphone,* a form of uni-directional microphone deriving its name from the heart-shaped field of pick-up. (3) *Condenser microphone,* one in which the diaphragm forms one conductor of a condenser whose capacitance is varied by the action of sound waves upon the diaphragm. The varying reactance introduces the current variations delivered as speech signals. (4) *Crystal microphone,* one in which the operation depends on the principle that certain crystals develop electric charges on certain surfaces when subject to the mechanical stress imposed by sound waves. (5) *Directional microphone,* one in which the sensitivity varies with the direction of the sound source. (6) *Lapel microphone,* a small microphone which can be fixed to a coat lapel. (7) *Moving-coil microphone,* depending for its operation on the current induced by a coil placed in a magnetic field through vibrations imposed on it by sound waves. (8) *Unidirectional microphone,* one which is sensitive only to sound coming from one direction. (9) *Velocity microphone,* one consisting of a light, corrugated metal ribbon suspended between the poles of a magnet. Sound waves strike the ribbon and cause its vibration, thus causing a current to be induced in it. Known also as a *ribbon microphone*.

MICROPHONE BOOM. Slang term, *mike boom*. See *Boom*.

MICROPHONE SHADOW. A shadow caused by the microphone entering the path of light or lights being used to illuminate the scene or shot.

MICROWAVE LINK. A high-frequency relay unit to transmit picture from a television mobile unit on location to the studio, or in connection with coaxial cable link-up.

MINIATURE. See *Model*.

MIRROR SPOT. A form of illuminator incorporating a mirror to concentrate the beam of light.

MIX. (1) Optical: see *Dissolve*. (2) Sound: to re-record several separate sound film tracks on to one main track. Often known as *re-recording;* also by slang term: *dubbing*.

MOBILE UNIT. Movable television equipment housed in a truck, or trucks, used for outside broadcasts such as sports, a telecast from a theatre stage or a special event.

MODEL. (1) Small-scale replica of a set made by art department for experiment and discussion with the director and other technicians before it is constructed full-size on the studio-floor. (2) Miniature model used in a television programme or film giving the illusion of a full-sized construction which is too costly or impracticable to erect in the studio. See also *Special Effects*.

MODELLING LIGHT. Illumination so arranged as to reveal the contours or texture of an object or person in close-up.

MODEL-SHOT. Television or film shot in which models are used instead of actual constructions. See also *Special Effects*.

MODULATION. A variation from a mean. In film recording, it represents a variation from a mean area or density (i.e., from a mean transmission). In variable area recording it appears as a peak or series of peaks photographically reproduced on the sound track.

MONITOR. Television receiver used in a control-room or on studio-floor to show the progress of a programme. By using several monitors at once, one for each camera channel, the director or producer in the control-room can guide the progress of his production and his technical staff can follow the action taking place on the studio-floor.

MONTAGE. An assembly of short film or television scenes usually linked together by dissolves, giving an impression of a lapse of time, or indicating the passage of several events. Note: not to be confused with original use of the word, meaning *editing*, as coined by Soviet film-makers in the 1920's and later used by European film-makers.

MOOD MUSIC. Background music to interpret the mood or atmosphere of the action of a scene.

MOSAIC. The photo-sensitive plate in an Iconoscope camera television tube.

MUSICAL. Type of light entertainment programme or film of which a large proportion is music and dancing.

MUTE NEGATIVE. Picture negative of film without sound track.

MUTE PRINT. Positive picture print without sound track taken from the negative film.

N. NARRATOR. An off-screen voice speaking commentary for a television programme or film. Also *commentator*.

NEGATIVE. (1) Raw film stock coated with a sensitized emulsion to record negative images when exposed to varying light intensities. (2) Negative film stock exposed but not processed. (3) Film bearing a negative image which has been developed by the laboratory.

NEGATIVE CUTTING. Cutting of the original negative, sound and picture of a film to match the edited positive prints, shot by shot, frame by frame, from which a combined print can be struck. Known also as *matching negative*.

NEMO (American). Slang term for a telecast from a location other than a television studio. See also *Outside Broadcast, Remote*.

NETWORK. A number of television or radio stations linked together by coaxial cable or relay stations for the wide transmission of programmes. (E.g., the National Broadcasting Company (N.B.C.), the Columbia Broadcasting System (C.B.S.), the American Broadcasting Company (A.B.C.) in the United States; the B.B.C. with its several transmitters in the United Kingdom also constitutes a network.)

NIGGER. Slang term for a screen used on the studio-floor or on location to cover or to reduce the amount of light from a strong illuminator. See also *Gobo*.

NON-THEATRICAL. A term used to denote the distribution of a film to audiences other than at public cinemas: e.g., to specialized audiences at film societies, universities, community organizations, clubs, etc. Such distribution is frequently by 16 mm. projection. Many film libraries exist to supply this market. Note: the term *non-theatrical* does not necessarily infer non-entertainment.

NUMBER-BOARD. A board showing the title of the film, the scene and take numbers, etc., which is held momentarily before a film camera and photographed at the beginning of a take, thus facilitating identification during editing. See also *Clapper-board*.

O. OFF-MICROPHONE. Of a source of sound; directed away from a sensitive face of a microphone. E.g., so as to convey an impression of distance. Slang: *off-mike*.

OPTICAL. A trick effect made mechanically in the laboratory to combine two or more film pictures into one by superimposition; thus used to produce *dissolves, fades, mixes* and *wipes*. Used colloquially to denote all these continuity devices.

OPTICAL PRINTER. (1) Apparatus used in film laboratory to combine film images for the making of opticals. (2) Apparatus used to make reduction prints from 35 mm. film.

OPTICAL SYSTEM. The combination of lamps, lenses and modulator or photo-electric cell used in recording or reproducing sound on film.

OSCILLATION. (1) Acoustics: vibration. (2) An alternating electric current, which may be at any frequency, e.g., an audio frequency, a video frequency, a radio frequency, and may be maintained by an oscillator or may occur fortuitously in an amplifier in which there is retroaction between output and input.

OSCILLATOR. An instrument for producing pure-tone electric waves callibrated on a frequency scale.

OSCILLOGRAPH. Synonymous with *galvanometer* for film-recording.

OSCILLOSCOPE. The signal received on each monitor in the control-room showing the comparative light values of black and white in the picture from each television camera in the studio or on location.

OUTSIDE BROADCAST. A television programme transmitted from an actual location away from the studio. See also *Nemo*, *Remote* (American).

OUT-TAKES. Film shots rejected by the editor in the cutting-room as being unsuitable.

OVERLAY. An electro-optical method of superimposing a television foreground picture on top of a second, background picture.

OVER-RUN. When a television programme runs over its scheduled length of time on transmission.

OVERSHOOT. To modulate sound track beyond the normal maximum amount, thus introducing distortion.

P.

PACKAGE (American). Slang term for a television film programme or series of programmes ready-made for transmission and available for purchase by an advertiser.

PAN or PANNING (*abbrev.* of panorama). The slow lateral movement of a television or film camera from left to right, or vice versa, across a scene, the camera set-up remaining stationary. See also *Tilt*.

PARALLEL DEVELOPMENT. A method of narrative construction in a film story or television programme in which the simultaneous development of two pieces of action is represented by showing short sections of each alternately.

PEAK PROGRAMME METER. An instrument designed to measure the volume of programme in a sound channel in terms of peaks averaged over a period of not more than one-hundredth of a second.

PEDESTAL (American). Movable studio camera-mounting, without boom arm, used usually by one operator.

PERFORATIONS. Holes punched at regular intervals down both sides of 35 mm. negative or positive film to let it be drawn over the driving-sprockets of the camera or projector. They are used by the claw-mechanism for the film to be pulled over the gate of the camera or projector frame by frame. Known also as *sprocket holes*.

PETITS DROITS (Legal term). Performing rights in symphonic and non-dramatic musical works.

PHASE (IN-PHASE, OUT-OF-PHASE). When a film camera or projector shutter is running in correct register with the intermittent action of the film. When the above action is not in register, the shutter and film are said to be out-of-phase.

PHOTOCELL AMPLIFIER. An amplifier designed to increase the amplitude of the minute signals from the photocell.

PHOTOELECTRIC CELL or PHOTOCELL. A valve in which the cathode is coated with a light-sensitive material so that the flow of electrons from cathode to anode is controlled by the amount of light allowed to fall on it.

PHOTOFLOOD. Light bulb giving a high-intensity light by its filament being subjected to very strong voltage; used for small locations with mains electricity supply.

PHOTOMETER. An instrument for measuring in foot-candles the intensity of direct or reflected light. See *Light-meter*.

PICK-UP. An electro-magnetic device for transforming the mechanical vibrations imparted by the modulated groove of a disc into alternating current.

PLAY-BACK. (1) The reproduction on a closed circuit of a recorded programme or of recorded programme material. (2) The reproduction of programme material, either live or recorded, through a loudspeaker in a studio, for the purpose of including such material in the sound picked up by the microphone, or for the purpose of enabling accompanying action of the actors to be synchronized with it.

POSITIVE. A print from exposed negative film.

POST-SYNCHRONIZATION. Recording and adding sound, speech or music to a film after the picture has been shot.

PRACTICAL. (1) Of a property, required to work in the manner of the real thing. (2) In a scene, an electric-light fitting which is required to work.

PRE-AMPLIFIER. An amplifier designed to function ahead of a main amplifier and amplify low-level signals sufficiently to be handled by the main amplifier.

PRE-EMPHASIS. The intentional increase in the relative depth of modulation of a transmission over a part of the frequency band, intended to be followed by the inverse process in reception so as to improve the signal-to-noise ratio over that part of the frequency band; a similar process applied to sound recording.

PRINT. See *Positive Print*.

PROCESS. To develop exposed negative film of sound or picture and to strike a positive print from same.

PROCESS SHOT. A film or television scene combining real photography with a back-projected background, or with models or other trick effects. See also *Model Shot*.

PRODUCER. In film and most television production, the executive individual responsible for the overall quality and other values; usually involved in the financial aspects of the production. In the B.B.C. Television Service the term " producer " is often used as synonymous with " director." See also *Director*.

PROGRAMME. (1) A self-contained item (play, talk, documentary, etc.) or self-contained selection of related items (concert, variety programme, etc.) for telecasting. Hence *programme building*, the action of choosing and arranging a number of items to form a programme. (2) A series of self-contained items collectively planned for telecasting from one station or network to comprise a day or evening's television viewing. Hence *programme planning*, the action of choosing and arranging a series of programmes to make up the output over a period of telecasting from a station or network. See also *Sponsored Programme, Sustaining Programme, Telecast*.

PROJECTION-TV. A system of presenting a television picture by a lens-and-mirror method on to a large screen in the home or in a cinema. Known also as *Big-screen television*.

PROJECTOR. An electrically-driven machine to produce a large picture on a screen from a film. See also *Flying-spot Projector, Mechau, Telecine Projector, Telecine.*

PROMPT KEY. A switch that allows the television sound channel to be interrupted in order that a prompt may be given unheard by viewers.

PROPERTIES. Articles and materials required in a scene for a film or television programme, e.g., furnishings, ornaments, pictures, fittings, drapes, etc. Slang term: *props.* See also *Hand Props.*

PROP PLOT. Detailed list of properties for a film or television programme usually drawn up by the head property man under directions given by the art director.

R.

RACK. To adjust a film projector or a telecine machine so that the upper or lower margins of the film frame do not show on the screen. Hence: *rack-up, rack-down.*

RADIATION. (1) Emission of electro-magnetic waves. (2) Energy emitted in the form of electro-magnetic waves.

RADIO FREQUENCY. See *Frequency.*

RATING (American). A method of measurement to estimate the size of an audience viewing a given programme and its reactions to same, computed on a " sample " method, of which there are numerous variations. Trade-names: Hooper, Nielson, Pulse, Trendex, Videodex. etc. The B.B.C. has its own Audience Research Department.

REAR-PROJECTION (American). See *Back-projection.*

RECTIFIER. A unit whose function is to allow current to pass in only one direction and which is thus capable of turning alternating current into direct current.

REDIFFUSION. The reproduction in public by means of a television viewing screen of a televised programme; a public showing of television.

REFLECTOR. Portable reflecting surface, usually silver in colour, to reflect light on to the object being photographed. For exterior work, reflectors are used to direct sunlight or artificial light on to the required action. For interior lighting, they are usually incorporated in the lamp-housing to reflect light from the back of the bulb.

RELEASE PRINT. Combined film print used for distribution to cinemas or to a television station.

REMOTE (American). See *Outside Broadcast.*

REPEAT. A television programme that is repeated either by using a telerecording (or kinescope) of the original performance, or by a re-telecast of the live programme.

REPRODUCTION. (1) Sound recording: the process by which the variations impressed on a recorded disc, or the modulations recorded photographically on to film, or magnetically on to tape, are converted into variations of an electric current corresponding to the wave-form of the sound recorded. Hence the application of this process, e.g., to a recording made either on a closed circuit or from a live telecast. See also *Play-back.* (2) The conversion of audio-frequency currents into sound waves by means of a loudspeaker. (3) The conversion of video-frequency currents into images formed on a television viewing screen.

RE-RECORD. To make a sound record by electrical means from one or more sound records, especially to make by electrical means a single combined track from several component sound tracks (dialogue, music, effects, etc.) of a film. See also *Dub, Mix*.

REVEAL. Of scenery, the side-thickness of an opening or recess.

REVERBERATION PERIOD. The time taken for reverberant sound at a particular frequency to decay by sixty decibels (i.e., to one-millionth of the original intensity) after the emission of sound from the source has ceased; (colloq.) the time taken for the sound to become inaudible.

REVERSE SHOT. The same object or person seen in shot by a second camera from an opposing angle to that used by the first camera. This can only be cheated in live television production because each camera will pick up the other.

RIG. To set overhead lights for a set in the studio, or on location.

ROSTRUM. A platform for use in a scene, or upon which to build scenery, available in a series of standard heights and sizes, collapsible when not in use.

ROUGH-CUT. The first edited but overlength assembly of film shots in their correct order and sequence according to script instructions.

ROW. A piece of scenery in the form of a low cut-out masking the bottom edge of a backcloth or other piece of scenery. Hence : *ground-row, mountain-row, tree-row*.

RUN-THROUGH. Usually the first complete rehearsal of a television programme by cast with cameras, sound, sets, music, etc.

RUN-UP. Footage which passes through the gate of a film camera or projector before it reaches the correct speed for filming.

RUSHES. Rushed prints : the first prints of film picture and sound, normally available not later than the day after they have been shot.

S. SATELLITE STATION. A subsidiary television transmitting station that takes vision signals by direct radio reception from a main station and rebroadcasts them on a frequency channel different from that used by the main station. See also *Booster Station*.

SCAN or SCANNING LINE. The separation by electronic means of the visual image on a television screen into a number of parallel horizontal lines running from left to right in sequence and from top to bottom of screen. Various countries have adopted, or are about to adopt, differing numbers of line-definition. Those known are as follows : 405-lines—United Kingdom; 525-lines—Alaska, Brazil, Canada, Colombia, Cuba, Hawaii, Japan, Mexico, Philippines. Puerto Rico, United States, Uruguay; 625-lines—Argentine, Australia, Austria, Belgium, Bulgaria, Czechoslovakia, Denmark, Germany (East and West), Hungary, Iraq, Italy, Netherlands, Poland, Sweden, Switzerland, Union of Soviet Socialist Republics, Venezuela, Yugoslavia; 819-lines—Algeria, France (and 441), Luxembourg, Monaco, Morocco, Saar, Tunisia.

SCENERY DOCK. Storage place where scenery is received and/or stored when not in use in the studio.

SCENIC ARTIST. Craftsman who paints scenery, backcloths, etc., sometimes of his own design but more often from a sketch supplied by the art director.

SCRATCH PRINT. Slang term for a positive film print supplied of a stock shot scored down the centre of the emulsion to prevent it being used as a duping-print without a fine-grain positive being ordered and the required royalty paid.

SCRIM. Mesh screen placed in front of an illuminator to diffuse its rays of light. See also *Diffuser, Jelly.*

SCRIPT. The text of a television programme or film, containing the words to be spoken, directions to those taking part and to technicians. Often used as an overall term to embrace several stages of writing such as: *synopsis* or *outline, treatment, master scene-script, camera-script, shooting-script.* (The term *scenario* is largely obsolete.)

SENSITOMETRY. The science of measuring the response of light-sensitive materials and the investigation of their behaviour under development.

SET-UP. See *Camera Set-up.*

SIGNAL. Acceptable transmission and reception of television picture and sound.

SINGLE-SYSTEM. Sound and picture recorded on the same piece of negative film simultaneously by one camera. See *Double-system.*

SNOOT. Slang term for an adjustable fitting applied to an illuminator so as to vary the size and shape of the cross-section of the beam. See also *Barn Door.*

SOAP-OPERA (American). Slang term for serial programmes, full of clichés and stock situations, telecast on five consecutive days weekly for 15 minutes' duration. The term is derived from the fact that the sponsors of such programmes are traditionally the soap manufacturers.

SOUND EFFECTS. Sounds other than dialogue, music or narrative recorded on a sound track of film, or on a disc or tape, used during re-recording process of film-making or during transmission of a television programme.

SOUND RECORDIST or ENGINEER. Technician concerned with recording and reproduction of sound (or audio) part of television programme or film.

SOUND TRACK. The narrow area running alongside the picture on the film on which are recorded the light variations which comprise the sound record.

SPACING. Raw stock, not usable for other purposes, used to separate sound tracks from each other in a rough-cut copy of a film. Known also as *blank spacing.*

SPEAK-BACK. See *Circuit, Talk-Back.*

SPECIAL EFFECTS. (1) Miniatures, dioramas and various optical devices used to give illusion of large settings impracticable or too costly to erect in the studio. (2) Trick devices made electronically in television or on the optical printer in film creating distortion with space and time. Hence: *special effects department, special effects man.* See also *Inlay, Model, Overlay.*

SPILL LIGHT. Light spreading from one scene or set on to another to upset the light balance on the second.

SPILL RING. An attachment fitted to an illuminator and comprising a series of concentric bands of a material having a non-reflecting surface so arranged as to interrupt rays other than those parallel to the optical axis of the beam of light.

SPLICE. To join together two strips of film, negative or positive, with special cement; also used to describe the join itself. Hence: *splicer*, a machine which makes film joins, either manipulated by hand or by electric power.

SPLIT FOCUS. To adjust focus of a television or film camera lens between two objects so that both foreground and background are in part focus.

SPONSORED PROGRAMME. A television programme the cost of which is paid for by an advertiser or other source of finance than the station or network. See *Sustaining Programme*.

SPOTLIGHT. An illuminator producing a highly concentrated beam of light.

SPROCKET-HOLES. See *Perforations*.

STAGE. See *Floor*.

STAGE MANAGER. Usually the chief assistant to the director, or producer, on a television programme acting as main link between him and the action taking place on the studio-floor. See *Floor Manager* (American).

START MARK. (1) A mark inscribed on the leader of a film to indicate the correct place for threading a projector. (2) Also for ensuring synchronism between picture and several sound tracks.

STATION BREAK (American). The transmission times between programmes, usually at 15-, 30-, 45- and 60-minute intervals, during which the television station is required legally to give its call letters, channel number and location, with such advertising as it has booked. In American television, the overall time of such a break is 30 seconds. Known also as *station identification*. See also *Call Letters*.

STEREOPHONIC. The property of having depth and direction in sound.

STOCK or RAW STOCK. Unexposed negative or positive film.

STOCK SHOT. A film shot from an existing film or from a library of such shots, supplied at a charge for incorporation in a new film or television programme. Most newsreel companies carry large libraries of such stock shots, as also do national archives, official film collections, etc. Hence: *library shot, library material*.

STOP-MOTION. Film taken by exposing one frame singly at a time instead of a number of frames continuously and intermittently exposed. Used mainly in *animation*.

STORY BOARD (American). A series of drawings laid out to show a development of a story for a television commercial programme or film so that an advertiser or sponsor, uninitiated in such techniques, can grasp what it is about.

SUB-STANDARD. Film of narrower gauge than the standard 35 mm.; usually 16 mm., 9.5 mm. or 8 mm.

SUPERIMPOSITION. The overlapping of a visual image produced by a television camera on the image produced by a second camera. Achieved in film-making by use of an optical printer.

SURFACE NOISE. Unwanted noise due to granular structure of the film.

P

SUSTAINING PROGRAMME (American). Unsponsored television programme put on by the station or network owning the the studio itself.

SWITCHER (American, slang). See *Technical Director*.

SYNCH. (IN-SYNCH.; OUT-OF-SYNCH.) (*abbrev.* for *synchronization*.) Slang term for synchronization of picture and sound tracks in film. If sound or picture is not exactly in register, it is known as out-of-synch. Sometimes spelt sync.

SYNCHRONIZED PRINT. See *Combined Print, Married Print*.

SYNCHRONIZER. An apparatus used in a cutting-room during editing a film, consisting of a set of sprocket-wheels, combined with rewinders, over which the sound tracks and picture can be run separately but kept in synchronization. Usually made in pairs or sets of four, hence slang term *two-way, four-way*.

T. TALK-BACK. (1) Circuit by microphone and earphones (cans) from producer or director in control-room to technicians and cast on the studio-floor during television rehearsals. (2) Telephone communication from mobile control-room to camera crew on location for outside broadcast used for cueing, etc. See also *Circuit, Speak-Back*.

TALLY LIGHT. See *Camera Cue*.

TAPE or TAPE RECORDING. Varying the impressed magnetic flux from a mean value according to the signal being recorded on a tape of film consisting of a plastic, paper or cellulose acetate base coated with a ferrous material which accepts the magnetic field and retains it until erased, or " wiped." Used widely for obtaining location sound effects and wild-tracks.

TECHNICAL DIRECTOR (American). See *Vision Mixer*.

TELECAST. (1) Of a programme: transmitted by means of television. (2) To transmit signals in the form of pictures and sound by the radiation of electro-magnetic waves for general reception by means of receiving-sets.

TELECINE. Term used to denote projection of film inserts or sequences into live transmission. See *Flying-spot Projector, Mechau Telecine Projector*.

TELEFILM (*abbrev.* for *television film*). A film made primarily for television transmission but which can also be shown by normal cinema methods. (Note: not to be confused with a telerecording or kinescope.)

TELEPROMPTER (American: *patented trade-name*). A mechanical device used in television production for visually prompting performers, announcers, public speakers, etc. The text of their speech is presented in big type beside. above or below the camera and moved vertically by electric control at a speed appropriate to the delivery of the speaker. See also *Idiot Sheet* (American).

TELERECORDING (*abbrev.* for *television recording*). The recording on 35 mm. or 16 mm. film of a television programme from the tube itself made either during an actual transmission or on a closed circuit (pre-telecording). See also *Kinescope* (American).

TELEVISION CAMERA. An apparatus in the shape of an enclosed case or box, into which light is admitted through a lens, forming an optical image of a scene and producing, by a process of scanning, electric currents at video frequencies corresponding to the image.

TELOP (American: *trade name*). An apparatus for projecting pictures of inanimate opaque slides or photographs for transmission by television. See also *Balop* (American).

THEATRE-TV. A television programme transmitted by closed-circuit on to a cinema screen to a paying audience. See also *Projection-TV*.

THROW. The distance between a film projector and the screen.

TILT. The vertical up-and-down movement of a television or film camera on its mounting or tripod. See also *Pan*.

TITLE or CREDIT TITLE. Name of television programme or film and credits of cast, producers, technicians, etc., which may be made on film, lettered cards or slides for television production. See also *Billing, Caption, Credits, Creeping Title*.

TOLL-TV. A method of television transmission and reception where the viewer pays to see a particular programme which he "unscrambles" either by placing a coin in the slot or by other method of payment. Known also as *Fee-TV, Pay-As-You-See TV, Pay-TV, Subscription-TV*. Trade-names: Phonevision (Zenith Radio Corporation), Subscriber Vision (Skiatron Electronics and Television Corporation), Telemeter (Paramount Pictures Corporation through subsidiary International Telemeter). Slang term for "unscrambling" the signal: pig-squeal TV.

TONE. The brightness of a particular area in a monochrome picture.

TOP-HAT. See *High-hat*.

TRACK-LAYING. The arrangement of one or more sound film tracks, bearing recordings of speech, music or sound effects so that they are in desired synchronization with the picture film. Operation carried out usually on a synchronizer in the cutting-room.

TRANSCRIPTION. (1) The verbatim script of a text of television programme as transmitted. (2) The recording of a live television programme by telerecording a film for despatch to one or more television organizations and for subsequent use by them. See *Telerecording*.

TRANSFORMER. An apparatus used in alternating current work con sisting of more than one winding of wire on an iron or iron alloy core. Variations in current in one winding induce corresponding variations in the other, the voltage depending upon the number of turns. An increase or decrease in the resulting voltage may thus be obtained.

TURKEY (American). Slang term for a flop or failure.

TURRET. A revolving mounting for television or film camera lenses to permit rapid change from one lens to another. See also *Lens-turret*.

U. UNMODULATED TRACK. A section of sound track on which no sound has been recorded which has a ground level in balance with the system of track being used elsewhere in the film. It is placed by the editor in between sound, speech or music when no sound is required during re-recording. Known also by slang term *buzz-track*.

V. VARIABLE AREA. The system of recording sound on film in which the track area is divided into two portions, the one clear and the other opaque.

VARIABLE DENSITY. The system of recording sound on to film in which the track is of uniform density across its width but in which

211

the transmission power of the track is varied from instant to instant along its length.

VARIABLE FOCUS LENS. A lens of which the focal length can be changed during shooting by a mechanism that alters the distance between front and back components of the lens. See also *Zoom*.

VAULT. Store or storage space for film constructed so as to conform with the safety regulations issued by the public authority.

VIDEO. The visual or picture part of a television programme or production as distinct from the audio, or sound, part.

VIDEO DIRECTOR (American). Also known as *technical director*; slang, *switcher*. See *Vision Mixer*.

VIDEO FREQUENCY. See *Frequency*.

VIDEO TAPE. The recording of pictures as well as of sound on magnetic tape, thus eliminating use of celluloid film and permitting immediate playback without laboratory processing. (Note: this process is still in an experimental stage.)

VIEWER RESEARCH. See *Rating*.

VIGNETTE. A mask placed in front of a television or film camera lens to give a picture in which only a selected portion is visible in a diffused oval or other shape as desired.

VISION MIXER. Technician in charge of the vision mixing-panel in control-room of television studio who makes changes of picture from one camera to another at the instructions of the director or producer. Also *video director* (American).

VOLTAGE AMPLIFIER. An amplifier whose primary function is to increase the amplitude of the input voltage without necessarily delivering a large power output.

VOLUME. The magnitude either of programme or of noise at a point in a sound channel, expressed in decibels relative to a standard reference volume according to the peak readings of a programme meter, the characteristics of which must be specified in order to define the volume accurately. See also *Level*.

W. WALKIE-LOOKIE (American). Slang term for small, portable television camera operated by batteries which can be carried around by one operator.

WAVE. A progressive rhythmical disturbance propagated either through a material medium (e.g., as sound waves are) or through space, whether containing or devoid of matter (e.g., as electro-magnetic waves are). Hence: (1) *Electro-magnetic wave*, a mode of propagation of electric and magnetic disturbances through space (e.g., radio waves, light waves). (2) *Long wave*, an electro-magnetic wave of more than about 1,000 metres in length. (3) *Medium wave*, an electro-magnetic wave between 100 metres and 1,000 metres in length. (4) *Short wave*, an electro-magnetic wave between 10 metres and 100 metres in length. (5) *Ultra-short wave*, an electro-magnetic wave between 1 and 10 metres in length.

WILD-TRACK. Sound which has been recorded separately from picture either on film, or on tape or disc.

WIPE. (1) Transition from one television scene or film shot to another by which a new shot replaces the old one in a moving, two-dimensional pattern (such as a square, circle, flip-over, iris, diagonal, etc.). In film it is made by an optical printer; in television by special electronic apparatus. See *Inlay, Overlay*. (2) Slang term for cleaning, or erasing, sound from a tape-recording for re-use of tape.

WORK-PRINT (American). See *Cutting-copy*.

WOW. A slow variation of frequency in the reproduction of recorded sound caused by a cyclic irregularity in the speed of the recording or of the reproducing mechanism, the audible fluctuation so produced being recognizable as a variation in pitch. See also *Flutter*.

Z.

ZIP PAN. Effect obtained by swinging a television or film camera very fast from one object to another so that between the two the picture on the screen is a blur.

ZOOM. The fast action of a continuous change in focal length in a special lens which gives the impression that the television or film camera itself has moved rapidly up to the object being photographed, whereas in actuality it has remained stationary. It is a device much used for sports events and in newsreels.

INDEX

215

THE TECHNIQUE OF FILM EDITING

Edited by Karel Reisz

288 pages, 181 photographs, 25 diagrams

Price 30/- (Postage 1/1d.)

Fourth edition

The *British Film Academy* set up a committee of ten distinguished and experienced film-makers and asked them to pool their knowledge in this work: *Reginald Beck, Roy Boulting, Sidney Cole, Thorold Dickinson, Robert Hamer, Jack Harris, David Lean, Ernest Lindgren, Harry Miller* and *Basil Wright*. What they have produced is more than a conventional text-book. It is a compendium of the views of Britain's leading directors and editors—not a statement by theoreticians. Its arguments are based on practical examples. It offers no hard-and-fast rules but states the problems of film-montage as they arise in practice. Being practising film-makers, they have made " The Technique of Film Editing " an essentially practical guide to their craft. The book is thus a unique survey of the central creative problem of film making and as such will prove indispensable to professionals and amateurs, connoisseurs and students of the cinema alike.

FOCAL CINE BOOKS

120-184 pages, 55-146 diagrams

Price 7/6 each (Postage 9d.)

Focal Cine Books tell the secrets of making good films. Focal Cine Books map out commonsense ways to the art of the amateur. Focal Cine Books are written by practical men who know the tricks of the great professionals and also how to make them easy, even for the budding amateur.

HOW TO FILM	HOW TO ANIMATE CUT-OUTS
HOW TO DIRECT	HOW TO SCRIPT
HOW TO USE 9.5 mm FILM	HOW TO WRITE FILM STORIES
HOW TO MAKE 8 mm. FILMS	HOW TO WRITE COMMENTARIES
HOW TO USE COLOUR	HOW TO PROCESS
HOW TO ADD SOUND	HOW TO EDIT
HOW TO CHOOSE MUSIC	HOW TO TITLE
HOW TO PRODUCE EFFECTS	HOW TO PROJECT
HOW TO DO TRICKS	HOW TO ACT
HOW TO CARTOON	HOW TO FILM CHILDREN

HOW TO MAKE HOLIDAY FILMS